Sexual Diseases Control

DR. Ebrahim Zamani

pencil

ISBN 978-93-5667-827-9
© DR. Ebrahim Zamani 2023

Published in India 2023 by Pencil

A brand of
One Point Six Technologies Pvt. Ltd.
Unit no. 26, Ground Floor, Building A1,
Wadala Truck Terminal Road,
Near Post Office, Antop Hill, Mumbai - 400037
E connect@thepencilapp.com
W www.thepencilapp.com

DISCLAIMER: *The opinions expressed in this book are those of the authors and do not purport to reflect the views of the Publisher.*

Author biography

The Author DR.Ebrahim Zamani has Published Many Medical Books such as Health, Medicinal Herbs ,Fitness and Diseases Control by Amazon and Other Publishers in English , German and French since 2010 as Read by Clinics and Patients.

CONTENTS

A Complete Guide to Women Medicine

A Complete Guide to Women Medicine
Sexual Diseases Control
Author: DR. Ebrahim Zamani
Parsian Medical Research Center

Vaginal diseases

A corridor that is stretched from the vulva to the neck or the wide part of the uterus is more affected by the cervix. Recurrent and persistent vaginal infections are usually observed in neck diseases. be. The measurement of the general state of the vagina should include the measurement of ovulation, the origin of which is the uterine cavity.

Trichomonas infestation

Trichomonas vaginal abscess as It has been seen that 15% or more of the women who have chosen a husband show different symptoms according to the duration of the disease. In some patients, greenish-yellow ovum discharge with many bubbles was observed, while in this group of patients, the part of the thigh that is close to the foreskin was red and tender, accompanied by itching and burning. It is abundant. The patient often wakes up from the pressure of his itch. despite pulling out the egg .

The egg continues to fall from the open uterus. The vaginal mucosa is red in color, soft, rough, with blood stains. The glands related to the urethra, the urethra and the vaginal vulva seem to be involved in gonorrhea. Like other vaginal cysts, the number of bacillus dodderlin decreases. In addition to these single cells, there are many leucocytes and bacteria. It is seen. The scope of this disease was different in a certain patient at different times and in individuals Different is infinitely variable.

The increase of symptoms and evidence is possible before menstruation, during. It is observed during or after menstruation. The diagnosis is different according to the type of egg shedding and it is based on finding motile single cells with fibrous and almond-shaped threads on unsetainable stains. Place one drop of egg on a slide, then mix it with two drops of natural salt water or pure water. Then immediately it. T ry it under a microscope placed in a relatively dark place..

Treatment:

How to treat trichomes attack is as follows. Phenylmercuric acetate - Nilmrite substance, Lorofin substance 4-Hydroxybenzenous acid and Hooking, patterning, cleaning agents - substance and liquid and mucus. The use of anti-trichomonas agents should be continued for two to six weeks.. Once every two weeks, in order to find out the result of the treatment, a careful examination should be done and if necessary Change the way of treatment. Monthly examinations are to ensure the rooting of the disease. Washing with water and acidification can be effective in healing and soothes the patient. forgive. Metrodinazol (Flagyl): which is prescribed orally, 250 mg two to three times a day for ten days, and it is very effective in preventing and suppressing this single cell. And it is useful. With this method of treatment, there is no need for topical treatment. Recurrence: Often, the source of re-infection starts from the person with whom they have sex. Treatment of defective or gland related to the urethra, vagina and cervix due to recurrence of infection. They turn. on chronic infection, treatment with metronidazole, or the use of Yzervator by the husband for a period of three months in the treatment and termination of the trichomonas infection.

It is necessary. Candidiasis(moniliasis) Candidiasis is common during pregnancy and is not always treated with diabetes.. Yeast composition like Candida (Monilia) albicans grows better in "serine" areas. Strong antibiotics may destroy normal bacteria and allow this seed to multiply. It is with abundant and unlimited itching. The vagina and clitoris are swollen and red. Small white spots remain on the vagina. Spores and the inner membrane of the egg can be removed on the sample stain and after adding 10% sodium hydroxide solution.

And the patches also show a small number of leukocytes. With better cultivation, this organism can be cleaned. In some rare cases, the patient emits a partial and watery discharge, which in the test and close examination, shines white. Vagina and shaft Zero has been observed in it. In such cases, the presence of spores and the inner membrane of the egg has been confirmed by microscopic tests on stains and sample pieces. Diagnosis is based on finding a living organism in the culture (Nickerson's method is excellent) along with observing the reaction of the factors that cause a pause in the growth of grain and meat. In undiagnosed cases, there may be a recurrence. It should be noted that Kasht is a Kasht Positive is usually possible from natural vagina, natural skin, or natural mouth..

Treatment:

To prevent the growth of Candida albicans(Monilia albicans is the name that some prefer.) The drug is used in the vagina for two weeks or more. Effective preparations include (1) vaginal mycostatin tablets (nystatin) and (2) propionac and nicotinic gel. (Gentiana Violet) 5% solution of Gentiana Violet may be prescribed by a doctor, but anyway.However, its reputation has been reduced due to repeated actions. 5% hydrocortisone cream solution in Faraj is usually the cause of visible relaxation. Pure water or acid shower gives temporary relief. In non-pregnant patients, it is not necessary to investigate whether the patient has diabetes or not. Glucose resistance tests are necessary to diagnose trichuria before taking the patient to the hospital. With the correct determination of cystic fibrosis, the candidate for Yazis treatment will be more successful. Elimination of Candida in the intestine by oral nisstatin infection from a man It may be necessary to prevent recurrence.

Haemophilus vaginal abscess

This type of swelling is caused by Haemophilus vaginal abscess, a bacteria identified by Herman Algardner and Sidi Dax.. The non-contagious chronic needle of women is gray in color and has a musty smell. Usually, the itching and burning is very partial or completely absent. In the example of a person, it goes to the heart of pus cells, and the cells of the mucous membrane are not very specific, but because of the bacilli appearing next to it. has it. This type of vaginal abscess is very common. Despite the existence of this part, there have been vaginal tumors that have been identified as "unknown". These bacteria may be seen with trichomoniasis. The husband usually has these bacteria in his gland secretions without having any symptoms, which should be treated. Vaginal treatment including triple sulfonamide cream or tetracycline with polymyxin ..

Vaginal Amas during old age

Defects and thinness of the vagina after menopause makes it less resistant to damage as a result of wound and infection.. The production of a skin wound on the thin mucous membrane may lead to adhesions if they appear in opposite points. If this situation is in the initial stages, the two walls can be separated easily, but if it is considered easy to treat, this adhesion is stronger. It has been and it is possible that it will cause steron and erase the vagina to some extent.. trichomoniasis, Candidiasis, vaginal abscess, hemophilus, and unknown bacterial infection may involve the ulcerated mucosa during aging.. In addition to the measures to treat the discomforts caused by topical estrogen and sometimes by mouth, estrogen treatment is to Ensuring that the mucus resists and the swelling continues..

Gonorrhea vaginal abscess

Neisseria gonorrhoea, when it is on the vaginal mucosa, usually becomes acute swelling after a few days.. In adult people, the soft tissue of the urethra, the vaginal gonads, and the uterine tube in the posterior part of the uterus are often the main focus of this reaction. When the discharge of abundant yellow liquid falls on the furnace, it is likely to cause burning, itching and tenderness. Urinary pressure and frequency of defecation are some of the symptoms. The action is the urinary tract. If the disease attacks the vagina and causes it to disappear, the pain will be extremely severe and it will cause swelling. Cut first in length and from. The lower part of the mucous membrane begins. In children and women who are older than. During menstruation, the infection rarely spreads from the posterior part of the uterus, however, during menstruation, acute inflammation of the endometrium or fallopian tube may occur.

Do not show unless treatment is necessary. Despite the fact that the cut is generally in the length of the membrane Mucosa is done, the unstable presence of bacteria in the blood can cause gout or swelling. Suzaki joints and heart endocarditis, which are the most important infections, should be effective.. This bacterium may have spread to the eye through the hand or other dirty transmission agents. Create a severe conjunctival abscess. Diagnosis: In children, any discharge with purulent fluid should be examined normally with the stain removal method. When you are in doubt about the presence of gonorrhea germs, the best way to remove the doubt is culture. Many women feel the discomfort and pain of gonorrhea, which is in the initial stages.

They endure their genitals as much as possible and when the pain of uterine tubercle pain comes to their heads, they think of a doctor and treatment.. Women may also be the cause of disease transmission. Accurate diagnosis requires diplocytic identification. Removal of pus from the mucous membrane of the vulva to the posterior part of the uterus or the urethra in acute cases without leaving a secondary effect of a large number of intercellular elements that cannot be stained by Gram's method.

It shows that, in general, dark spots remain in the white vaginal discharge.. During the incubation period (three to fourteen days) and in patients suffering from swelling of the posterior part of the uterus, uterus, and urinary tract, the stains are often undetectable. In semi-acute and chronic cases, repeated culture and examinations are necessary Fluorescent antibody. It guarantees effective and quick diagnosis in direct stains or stains resulting from new cultivation.. In chronic cases, you should look for chancre or anal warts. The validity of this topic depends on usage The use of penicillin is more proven because penicillin is really effective in the rapid relief of syphilis wounds.

It works wonders, but it may not be enough to kill spirochetes.. Mostly others Sexually transmitted diseases are seen in a woman suffering from gonorrhea.. The person from whom this disease has spread should be found and treated immediately. The one who has intercourse with him. It is treated earlier with preventive drugs. Treatment:

If the patient is not allergic to penicillin, this drug is very useful for treatment.600,000 units of procaine in the muscle is possible .It is a cure. Oxytetracycline, chlortetracycline and tetracycline are effective in 250 mg four times a day for five days. If syphilis is suspected, sulfadiazine or gantrycin 1 gram four times a day for six days or streptomycin 1 gram intramuscularly twice a day for five days may be prescribed and used to make a more specific diagnosis. These antibacterials have no effect on syphilis.. Chronic swelling of the posterior part of the uterus and uterus, Ascan's adenoma or Bartholin's adenoma may require cutting or destruction of the invaded tissue. The scale of treatment includes (1) the absence of disease symptoms and five months after examination and treatment, (2) the negative result of the culture of the posterior part after three or more times, (3) the absence of contagion in a man .who has intercourse with the woman in question. Gonorrhea in children is usually sensitive to antibiotics. Estrogen stimulation is rare. It is used to increase vaginal resistance..

The opposite of external factors

In cases of vaginal abscess in children, it should be due to the presence of external factors.. Touching the areas related to the right intestine and viewing the vagina with a proctoscope or general ureteroscope may be used. "Forgotten" or "overlooked" vaginal suppositories are likely in adults. The reason for that is the diaphragm or the wick.

Reactions of chemical reactions

As a result of pharmaceutical medicine or due to the effects of drugs that have been used to prevent pregnancy, it is possible that there will be a reaction in the vagina.. The purple gentian community and the particles of potassium permanganate pills are among the main attackers. Severe bleeding caused by this pill It has been used to abort the fetus, it has been seen a lot recently..

Amas

Vaginal pouches that are inserted in the side areas are usually of the type of duct pouches. They are Gartner. The pouches that have been seen in the outer quarter of the back wall of the vagina are mostly of the type. There are attached bags. Since these bags have no holes, they are rarely of origin. They become infected and rarely cause symptoms.. The accumulations are solid and hard.

Harmless vaginal .It can be treated like a bone. Cancers that we often face .They are secondary cancers. These displaced growths are possible. The cancerous tumor of the posterior part can also spread to other places, such as the cancerous tumor accompanied by glandular factors of the endometrium or the malignant tumor formed from the mucous membrane. Radiation is used.. Small-sized bags without a hole in cases where there is enough space in the urinary tract for the contents to pass cannot appear as accumulations and can be seen with trogography. A sac without a small hole may appear.. As a result, patients suffering from this. If there is any discomfort, they should be examined more carefully, and the only way to cure it is complete excision..

Pipe

The tube related to the bladder and vagina causes constant or intermittent urine dripping in the vagina.. Injury as a result of current surgical wound is one of the common discomforts that can be cured by diagnosing and repairing the wound on the bladder. In the past, injuries related to viability (surgery, difficult and prolonged childbirth, and infection) are common causes.

Dryness of the root or skin, removal of cancerous tumors or no radiation may be effective in the tube. Wounds caused by surgery or post-surgical blood supply cut off are. Recently, it is seen more and more with lymphatic displacement by surgery or uterine incision.. A tube related to the uterer and vagina or a tube related to the bladder and vagina may be the result of surgery or urine penetration of the posterior part or the cervix. The tube related to the right intestine and urethra after cesarean section causes menstruation through the bladder and the lack of penetration of the prostate in the posterior part of the uterus. Cystoscopy and urography are necessary for diagnosis.

These types of tubes may heal by themselves. In the absence of severe and dangerous radiation injuries, most of them can be treated with the necessary equipment and basic stitches. The tube related to the rectum and. The vagina is the cause of gas penetration, the liquid stool goes into the vagina.. Injuries caused by surgery and disability are common cases. Surgical repair is usually successful. The time to repair the genital tube that has a wound origin and is unable to heal itself depends on the length of time required for tissue swelling to subside.

With the necessary antibacterial agents and with the use of combined topical corticoids, this period becomes shorter. Anticoagulant is necessary And it is necessary to equip the tissues in order to prevent additional stimulation during suturing.. After repairing the bladder tube and vagina, you should use a catheter to prevent It should be kept empty from the stimulation in the place of the stitches until the time of treatment and sufficient healing..Tearing and laxity of the pelvic outlet. The parts related to the front part of the muscles together with the compressed muscles from the support. The main drains are pelvic.

Transverse muscles of civer related to Urinary and genital organs are located superficially to the frontal muscles and to Its maintenance force helps. The bulbocavernosus muscle is superficial compared to the onion. It is located and is included in the rule of the sphincter muscle.. The members of the holding structure usually include the entrance and the front part of the vagina, in this case, the vagina is in a sufficiently forward position. is located.

When the upper part of the vagina and the posterior part of the uterus are pushed back enough .As a result, the inner part of the abdomen is not stretched to the vaginal axis..

That is, this pressure It does not pass through the vaginal canal. sometimes due to injury as a result of an accident or An accident or violent adultery causes a tear, in any case, the main and general cause of it is the state of pregnancy.. Difficult or sudden extraction of surgical tools, the position of carrying due to haste and failure in the necessary repair are considered as the main factors.

To avoid pain, it is better to use episiotomy. Women who are under the close care of midwives rarely suffer from pelvic organ weakness. The area of gingival laceration, if it includes mucosal tissue and upper related tissue, is considered first degree. With a second-degree tear, the muscles of the mucous membranes are separated, and a third-degree tear includes the circular muscle. The injury that creates a wound in the body of the tooth can cause tearing of the muscles related to the bone. stretching and stretching of the vaginal organs and genitals.

Deficiency in exercise causes Muscles become weak and thin. When the entrance and the grain is expanded, with this expansion to fall It is from him. In fact, the internal pressure of the abdomen is more focused on the grain and output and sometimes results. It causes the anterior or posterior wall of the vagina to fall out.. In this case, intercourse is for None of these sides should be enjoyable.. Exercising the pubic bone and coccyx-related muscles for several weeks regularly will sometimes improve the support, but of course this is only if the tear is not deep. When an appreciable part of the penis is lost, the best treatment is a penis suture, but in any case, this suture is usually needed during subsequent childbirth or other genital surgery. Complete tearing of the ajajan (third degree) results in not having the ability to defecate. Today's midwifery science, 3rd degree molar tears are repaired and usually heal well. In case of delay in the repair, the operation has been successful.

Surgery made the related organ normal. With small anatomical changes, without bladder disorders and discomforts, or rectal and rectal procedures, surgery is not necessary. When the weak pressure in urine retention is the main discomfort, cystoscopy and cystography should be done before colporrhaphy for fear of ignoring cystic hemorrhoids, stone, unknown infection, nerve disorders. Anterior colporrhaphy is completed in the following order: (1) by separating the anterior wall of the vagina from the bladder and urethra, (2) by suturing the wall of the bladder in order to correct the defects of its progression and in the tissue next to the urethra and urethra and voluntary muscle fibers (for urethral prolapse defects) additional sutures for patch augmentation.

The sacral bone or the cervical part of the main joints should be used to add support to the wall. Sew the front of the vagina. If the area of the internal circular muscle of the urethra is high enough Stretched, weak pressure, urinary retention can usually be improved.. If the bladder hernia is repaired without adequate support of the posterior ureter, even though there is an effect of weak pressure. If there is no urinary retention, this discomfort is created. How to turn the back of the bladder .If the colporrhaphy does not return to its original axis or if a small medial hernia is observed after the pubic prolapse, ureterosicopexy may be used to cure weak urinary retention.. This break is possible by suturing the tissues near the urethra and bladder. The part of the vaginal wall is necessary.

Intestinal hernia(posterior vaginal hernia)

This type of hernia is an extension of the choledochal sac as a peritoneal sac between the rectum and the vagina, which may include the esophagus, small intestine, or complex vein.. Three types of intestinal hernia The order is as follows: 1- A rare congenital type in which the sac extends to the lower part of the peritoneal body. 2- Acquired type that appears either as a convexity in the upper part of the back of the vagina, usually above the advancement of the rectum in the vagina, or along with the prolapse of the vagina after cutting.

It is the womb. One of its symptoms is the feeling of pressure in the vagina or the appearance of accumulation in its entrance or channel. Its repair by surgery should close the bag and be able to use uterine grafts and sacral bones as a support. When it is necessary to repair other organs, they usually start from the vagina. with vaginal prolapse after hysterectomy or vaginal cleaning with surgery. It is possible to do sat and this is in the case that there is no more interest in intercourse when .The vagina should be kept to the main joints and the uterine joints and the necessary sacral bones. There is no strip of paper in the shape of the inner wall of the abdomen. Sometimes the original connected. season6 displacement of the uterus.

Explanation

The uterus is located approximately in the center of the pelvic cavity, and the body of this organ is inclined to the front, and its long axis is stretched towards the top of the pelvic joint, and this stretching is different in different people. and in addition, it varies in a single person and in different situations.. The uterus is never in a fixed position and can easily move in different directions. Up, down, front or back. When the bladder is full, this member is pushed back and the upper part is like that. If the rectum is full, it leans slightly forward. Therefore, the uterus can easily fluctuate in a wide range and only when it fluctuates beyond this range. You can say that the uterus has moved. What keeps the uterus in normal conditions?. The uterus is kept in a natural state by the following factors: (1) pelvic floor, (2) broad ligaments (the most important parts of which are the main joints), (3) uterine joints and sacral bones, (4) circular joints, (5) the natural state and position of the adjacent pelvic organs.

Backwardness

Uterine retrograde happens in two cases: Retroflexion (bending to the back of the uterus after It is obtained. Most backwardness is a combination of these two conditions. Scientific motivation. The reasons for the displacements are as follows:3- Uterine firmness may be due to the following reasons: A- Adhesion of peritonitis B- Disturbance of tissues in the pelvic cavity J- Pelvic cancer 4- Displacement occurs in the following cases: A- Bladder enlargement b- Endometrial swelling c- Ovarian tumor symptoms:

In patients suffering from hereditary translocation or post-pregnancy symptoms. The compression of the expansion of the uterus during pregnancy in the lower part of the uterus, depending on the sacral bone, may rarely be the cause of miscarriage or abortion of the fetus.. When a man's penis interferes with sexual intercourse, a woman feels terrible pain in the region of the ovaries and clavicle.

Pressure on the pelvis and back pain may be accompanied or without uterine fixation. Pay attention to the hysterectomy test. (Due to multiple factors, it is possible to attribute these symptoms to the displacement of the uterus after continuous and continuous examinations for a period of several months. The dilation of the uterine and ovarian cysts should also be taken into account.

Treatment:

The path of the cervical axis can be considered as the probable basis of the position of the uterine body, but for For sure, it is better to touch it with your hand. The ease of uterine movement is necessary to determine its causes. If the uterus is fixed, the disease that caused this can be considered as a clear example and the main cause of discomfort. Just as you can hold the uterus forward by touching it, and you don't notice any other symptoms of discomfort, you can close the uterus by lowering the uterus. kept it the same.

Test of the uterine band: If the patient feels relaxed within a month, the uterine band can be removed, and if the back pain or other discomforts come back to the patient, the uterine band will be inserted again and placed in the first place until it is known that The contraction of the uterus relieves the pain Accepted or not? By observing this test and pulling in and pulling out the uterus, it can be determined. Does the patient need to use it permanently or does he need hysteropexy?.

Treatment:

In some patients, a uterine band can be used. If pregnancy happens, the uterus should remain in the vagina until the uterus has grown enough and filled the empty sac of the sacrum. Knee-chest position may temporarily pull the uterus forward. Lying down may be effective in driving the uterus to the anterior position, especially during the first six weeks after pregnancy. When the uterus is compressed and contracted, the best method is for the patient to "stand on the balance" with the help of a nurse, because this method has been effective in cases of pregnancy or heavy and enlarged uterus compared to other methods that have been fruitless.

It is. Hysteropexy is rarely used in primary cases. Mostly to keep one. The freed uterus, which is fixed due to endometriosis or due to adhesions resulting from infection, is used for suspension.. Chinese erosion of uterine ligaments and sacral bones and shortening of circular ligaments by stretching them through the rings attached to the thigh and suturing them to the sheet. The inner rectus muscle is one of the most popular methods.

Falling out

Prolapse of the uterus is a condition in which the uterus moves from its natural level towards the pelvic cavity. It turns out that this state is also called Presidentia Otteri, but mostly by the name"Out Uterine prolapseIt is addressed to the patient. In a normal state, the prolapsed uterus is moved, the pelvic floor is torn, and frequent visits appear. The walls of the vagina are loosened and in the uterine position they become taut and it may move outward and towards the entrance of the vagina in the form of an anterior or posterior hernia. Bladder hernia and right advancement in the vagina are also accompanied by this discomfort. Cervical wounds may be due to stimulation of the lining and interference in blood circulation with third degree progression. Resistance to ulcers and recurrence of wounds along with.

The infection related to it may result in the formation of fibers and thickening of the outer wall of the vaginal prolapse.. All the ligaments of the uterus are stretched to the point where they practically lose their holding power and the lower pelvis is occupied by the intestines instead of the reproductive organs. Intestinal loops are possible It is located outside the entrance in Kaldosak and creates the rear advancement of Kaldosak.. outside Miscarriage can also happen to a woman who has never been pregnant.. Dryness of the pelvic joints and other tissues after menopause is due to estrogen stimulation, which causes an increase in uterine prolapse, so second and third degree prolapse is more common in older women. It is. The use of estrogen reduces the degree of prolapse in some patients.

Scientific motivation:

 damage as a result of the wound from carrying and drying of the main links and Cervical bone grafts are one of the main causes of prolapse.. The uterus usually has a range of motion in which it can easily move around. Breathing, especially blowing, causes the uterus to move, which can be clearly seen during the examination with a speculum or a light reflector, especially if the patient is in Sims' state. It is possible that abnormal swelling and disorganization can happen without seeing the symptoms, and in this case, the science of pathology cannot be blamed.. If there are not enough signs and evidence of irregularity, it cannot be called prolapse, and this prolapse is almost always accompanied by posterior uterine irregularity. The cervix may be elongated and narrowed to the point where the internal. The entrance appeared while the body of the uterus is also in its natural place.. If the cervix is right in the middle of the vagina, in this case it is called first degree prolapse. If the cervix is protruding from the vagina, this condition is called second degree. Finally, if the uterus has completely fallen out of the vagina and is hanging outside the body, it is third degree or out. They say a complete fall. Symptoms: Since the decline happens gradually, the symptoms of the attack of this disease also appear gradually. Many patients get used to the accumulation of this discharge and swelling. If there is no fear of swelling, they will never consult a doctor.. In the next stages of feeling Painful falling out of something inside the body happens to the patient.. Often bladder and anterior hernia. The painful arrival of the rectum in the uterus, which is accompanied by this disease, causes the symptoms to appear..

Treatment:

The sedation measures include cleaning the local fibroids by cleansing douches, systemic or topical estrogens, and using a uterine band to keep the uterus in the pelvic cavity.. If there is enough space in the pelvic cavity to keep the uterine band, one of the "doughnut" or "honeycomb" types of cervical band may be used. This type of uterus is used to block the outflow, while the uterus is used to keep the uterus in the front position. They become slaves by moving their body and cervix backwards and upwards, they also do the same thing.. Curative measures require surgery. Usually, the treatment has been accompanied with more decisive success in patients who are post-menstrual age or those who have put the desire of pregnancy behind. Vaginal hysterectomy, partial steronectomy, vaginal surgery and suturing, and vaginal suturing are effective. With complete surgical reduction and suturing of the vagina

Suspension

rolapse of the uterus is often accompanied by an acute illness, which is irregularly the third stage and labor pain, which can usually be placed in its natural place with the help of the hand.. Prolongation may be due to the stretching of the uterus by semimucous myositis through .May the neck of the womb be. Vaginal hysterectomy is usually necessary in case of acute prolapse. season7 Pelvic infections Pathogenic organs that cause pelvic abscess may enter the vagina through blood or lymphatic vessels, by direct extension of the organs inside the pelvic cavity, and by the spread of infection from other parts of the peritoneal cavity.. The vagina is one of the main factors of disease transmission in the vagina. B A system in pregnancy causes the creation of wounds and frequent cultivation for the generalization and reproduction of bacteria.. During the surgery, the infection may spread to other organs. The entry of foreign elements or neoplasms that cause the blockage of the vaginal canal may be spread by effective factors. Infection in the pelvis. Neck cancers often cause the growth of toxic bacteria. Chronic services may be a way for recurrent infection..

Amas Had Shipour Rahmi Despite the presence of effective antibacterial agents in gonorrhea patients as the main It is a womb. As mentioned in the fifth chapter, gonorrhea of the lower vaginal area is likely to appear mild and soft, especially with symptoms. With its development in the inner membrane of the uterus, it reaches the mucous membrane of the fallopian tube. Here, the cause of the formation of purulent exudation factors accompanied by amas is acute, with the gradual accumulation of high B amoeba exudation. The color of the waste appears in the tube wall.

 As long as the rooted end of the tube is open. The infection has spread to the ovaries and the adjacent peritoneum and causes pelvic peritonitis. will be. (Image) 17 The symptoms of this disease are pain, fever and chills, and may also be accompanied by nausea and vomiting. be. Specific peritoneal stimulation results in frequent tenderness with localized muscle spasm. Abdominal wall and acute pain appears when touching the neck area.. Often, this pain is identified with the attack of this disease in such a way that doctors are unable to correctly diagnose the pelvic organs. They stay. Examining the discharge from the neck and urinary tract at this time may be the cause.

 Treatment:

terine cystitis related to gonorrhea can be treated without definitive treatment by the affected woman herself, but this disease leaves long-term consequences and damage to the egg passage and adjacent organs.. The best way to treat gonorrhea-related uterine tube abscess is to prescribe penicillin 600,000 units of procaine daily until the patient's fever stops. be. Anesthetic agents are also effective in reducing pain. Usually.

The result will be updated immediately. If an acute uterine fibroid is seen in the uterus or abdominal cavity and It is necessary to take measures in the case of stains and pus, this disease can also be cured with medicine.. Different types of uterine cysts: If this disease is not treated in the early stages or if treatment is not necessary, it may result in a boil related to the fallopian tube and ovaries, a boil with pus storage in Egg passage or pelvic swelling. In some cases, when the disease pressure reaches this level, gonococcus is connected to streptococcus and coliform bacteria. With the secondary attack of the disease, the patient is suffering from acute unhappiness, and due to the cause of Ilaus, he develops abdominal distension, which is accompanied by confusion and vomiting, infectious fever and constant pain. The examination in such a description makes us face the pelvic organs too gently, where we may find huge accumulations here and there, and these accumulations are sometimes due to mobile accumulations in the cold sac or in the lung tissue. Complete antibacterial treatment is vital. Fluids outside the alimentary canal are often needed.

If the ileus colon leads to enlargement, gastric lavage is necessary. As soon as the boil is hit, it is better to dry it by choledotomy in the back part, and if you do not reach it with this surgical procedure and the boil remains attached to the abdominal wall, drying and draining it out of the peritoneal cavity by The cut depending on the thigh gap is absolutely necessary. As long as the swelling did not dry up and the treatment was ineffective, and this development still remains, it takes months and months to get rid of this type of boil. Oral administration of soluble yeast material of topical proteolysis may be effective in reducing the duration of treatment. When it comes to fallopian tubes and ovaries that cannot be removed.

The way of the abdominal wall or the back of the vagina is the best way to access the incision.. If you do not receive effective antibacterial treatment, surgery is necessary, and often this is combined with salpingo-oophorectomy and complete hysterectomy. Separating advanced swelling of fallopian tubes and ovaries, if possible, before it ruptures, because when these boils rupture, and with the number of patients dying, this operation is often necessary and is emphasized even above normal.

If the surgery is successful after tearing, in such a situation, the infection of the peritoneum cavity can be eliminated. After the development of a pelvic infection caused by a purulent fallopian tube cyst or a number of recurrences of a pelvic infection caused by a fallopian tube cyst. I have severe lower abdominal pain and back pain and irregular menstruation.. Softness, stiffness, closure and limitation of the range of uterine oscillations are often seen..

The decision to Surgical treatment for residual pelvic infection is better based on the assessment of the patient's disability.. Months should pass before making this decision. Efforts should be made in the treatment of the disease. Total skin hormone, if added to an effective antibacterial agent, may speed healing significantly. A warm shower will relax the patient. Bringing heat to body tissue by electric current is likely to be effective. Accumulations that remain after a pelvic infection may be an acute abscess of the fallopian tube and ovaries including steron, accumulation of pus in the egg passage, ovarian abscess, pelvic abscess, or an intestinal abscess. After months, it is possible to create an accumulation of aqueous fluid in the fallopian tube. These accumulations, which are the result of swelling, are likely to be mistaken for abnormal growth or tumors, and when these accumulations remain for months, even if the symptoms show, they need to be cut. It is.

Pelvic heel

This condition may not only be due to a purulent uterine tube abscess, but it may also be due to rupture of the rhyming appendix, rupture of gastric ulcer, nervous breakdown, illegitimate pregnancy accompanied by bleeding in the cavity, or internal operation of the abdomen.. Long-term fever after pelvic surgery leads a person to the diagnosis of pelvic abscess. A foreign object that remains in the inner part of the abdomen during surgery may be considered as a contributing factor.

As it was said in the grouping of these boils, drying is the best step after the fallopian tubes. If drying is not possible, for the purpose of treatment, it is possible to cut it by removing part or all of the boil. An effective surgery will take place. When the infection of the ovarian sac organs is obtained, this the situation. They say "Ovarian stew". These boils may be due to pelvic infection or in the sac. The abdominal cavity that protrudes from the inner wall is created.

Infections after miscarriage, childbirth and after surgery

After miscarriage or pregnancy, usually a short swelling appears in the inner lining of the uterus, which the body has repaired by itself and does not need treatment.. Following the use of reasons and Accessories or severe contamination of the uterus, the inner membrane of the uterus swells significantly.. The agents that cause this discomfort the most are Staphylococcus and Streptococcus, in addition to these, however, other agents may also be the cause of the invasion of this disease, including Clostridium and leech. The wall of the vessels and the occurrence of clots in the blood of the pelvic cavity.. Special softness in the movement of the uterus .It is observed and its hardness, which may be the hardness of wood, can be attributed to the interstitial tissue. Two layers of wide bond should also be stretched. Treatment: With lightning strikes, infections involving gram-negative bacilli are possible. Endotoxin is released and causes infectious shock.. Lower blood pressure and diameter narrowing Extravasations lead to venous return defects and renal blood circulation defects.. the patient.

There is a possibility that he sweats and suffers from blue jaundice or blue pain, vomiting, diarrhea and urine will be very less.. A vasopressor is needed to establish the necessary arterial pressure). (is recommended that there is no leakage of urine from the body. Separation of the peritoneal connection is possible with the use of "artificial kidney". If the infection is controllable and the damage to the kidney tissue has occurred, the patient should get better.. The patient should be treated with the necessary antibacterial agents.

Preliminary treatment with penicillin and Sufficient amounts of streptomycin for intramuscular injection, or effective drugs such as chloramphenicol, tetracycline, and oxytetracycline may be prescribed orally or as needed intravenously.. Patients who are suffering from this infection may show symptoms of anemia, and sufficient blood should be injected into this group of patients as soon as possible. Liquids outside the alimentary canal or food ampoule are necessary in case of disorders in the digestive system preventing sufficient absorption.

The result of the culture of certain factors from the uterus may be effective in identifying the main microbes. If the sick patient has tremors, a blood culture is also necessary. X-ray examination X-ray of the chest may be effective in the initial diagnosis of the defect caused by the vascular ligation infection.. In cases of vein blockage due to blood clotting or other factors, the use of anti-clotting agent is recommended. Clines, who has enough experience and experience in the field of such discomforts, proves that the closure of ovarian veins and arteries is often the cause of saving patients who were suffering from uncontrollable infections.

When the acute form of this discomfort subsides, the patient may suffer from frequent weakness accompanied by swelling of the pelvic ligaments. Oral administration of skin hormone and soluble proteolysis yeast along with strong antibacterial agents accelerates the reaction in the tissues. It is possible to create an abscess of the tissues and peritoneum around the fallopian tube, which results in a crooked tube, of course, it does not have symptoms and evidence as much as a pus-filled uterine tube abscess. In some of the cases of infection accompanied by myositis of the semimucosa, which is caused by external factors in the uterine cavity. They come and sell only after complete hysterectomy..

Tuberculosis related to reproductive organs

Tuberculosis in the pelvic organs is often secondary to injuries in other parts of the body.. Its first place may be lung, intestine, urinary tract, or retroperitoneal gland. Tuberculosis Peritoneum may include pelvic organs. Despite the fact that tuberculosis may start through the vagina, the way it spreads is usually through the blood producing organs. Most of the time Diagnosis of a specific wound is not visible in the initial stages.. The severity of the disease is completely variable. In the weaker stages, during the pelvic examination, we do not see any major discomforts or inconsistencies.

However, some of these cases can be recognized when there are tests about infertility.. A biopsy of the inner lining of the uterus leads to the diagnosis of tuberculosis.

Sometimes the diagnosis of tuberculosis is made when the patient is referred for the treatment of blood on the uterus. In some cases, tuberculosis results in a severe infection, in this case, peritonitis with dense hard adhesions. It causes adhesion of abdominal and pelvic .The uterus is attacked and then the inner membrane of the uterus and ovaries are at risk of attack. They are. Cervical sinuses, vagina, or vulva are rarely infected with chronic wounds.

The local symptoms indicate that the disease was in a chronic state, however, sometimes its acute state appeared and this discomfort is likely to be combined with other disorders and tumors of the pelvis.. It is rarely possible to diagnose the disease before surgery. When the defect and inability to diagnose in cases of abscesses and resistance to common treatments, the possibility of tuberculosis should be considered. It makes it stronger. The correct diagnosis of the disease depends on the diagnosis and purification of mycobacterium. Tuberculosis is accompanied by pus, culture, and inoculation of pigs.. Histological diagnosis.

It is enough to determine the classification of the disease. Treatment: If the diagnosis is made before surgery, the treatment of pelvic tuberculosis is the same as the treatment of tuberculosis in other parts of the body. Daily injection of 1 gram of streptomycin for three to six Mah, para-amino salicylic acid12 grams of isonicotinic acid hydrazide orally every day 300 grams daily or for several months can be taken together or only for several months. The possibility of pregnancy becomes very weak after drug treatment. The best way to treat the affected part of the genital organ is with surgery, especially with the above-mentioned drugs.

This chronic discomfort may also attack the pelvic organs.. Although this situation is very rare .It has been said that the diseased organ is inserted through the uterus, intestine or stomach.. It is possible as obtained and if this disease reaches the open bladder, the possibility of diagnosis. Its microscopy increases many times.

Treatment:

After removing the pelvic mass and diagnosing the disease, inject the compounds into the muscle. Long life of penicillin such as benzine penicillinG, 1,200,000 units per week for six or eight weeks is necessary if the cutting is not done enough. Ecoz Penicillin 2000000 daily units should be used for severe infections. Harmless wounds of the uterus.

 Cervical injuries

Hereditary corruption

Entering the cervix(the columnar mucous membrane) is stretched towards the prolapse of the uterus in the vagina so that the red area surrounds the inner cervix. One of the main symptoms before intercourse is excess mucus. These symptoms are symptoms in Mothers, it is possible that in the case of internal growth of candida or unpleasant bacteria, it will result in vaginal abscess. Cervicitis may appear after several times of regular intercourse. An increase in the amount of mucus may lead to vaginal abscess. increases or chronic cervicitis appears, it is necessary to remove the wound of the uterine cervix, which is otherwise .Naturally, it is set to burn.

 Return

Reversal of the uterus refers to the return of the entrance to the cervix, which is accompanied by tearing.. Almost the majority of patients are treated by burning with electricity.

If a few weeks after giving birth, a deep laceration is observed and you do not observe a wound or a harmful infection in the entrance of the cervix, the suture of the cervical laceration may be placed in its place and reduced. The return should be effective.

Servicing

Acute cervicitis often has a bacterial origin and its cause may be trichomoniasis or candidiasis.. The topical use of chemical drugs or antibacterial agents is usually effective. If the urethra, endometrium or fallopian tubes are attacked by this disease, treatment .It should be done by mouth or non-topical injection.. The service has been seen for a long time. It is. Cervical penetration is exposed to the vaginal part of the cervix, which is either an inversion due to tearing or corruption, which is vulnerable to recurrent infection.

A foreign body in the cervical canal (uterus of the peduncle) can cause an infection as a result of injury or miscarriage. Recurrence of sarcoidosis leads to changes in the organ. Vaginal prolapse is a symptom.

The discharge varies from yellow, purulent, to a mucus-like fluid.Pain or pressure in the lower part. Abdominal or back pain is likely to be a sign of lymphatic edema.. It is possible to touch the cervix Show the partial amount of blood loss. Chronic servicitis tolerates tension and temporary stimulation and relief. There is always mutual influence and action between the skin of the mucous membrane like a shape and a column. The skin of the mucous membrane is trying to cover the glands entering the cervix and block it so that the holding bags (Nabothians) are filled with mucus. When the number of holding bags increases, the cervix becomes loose. Cylindrical cells take the shape of the gland at the entrance of the cervix.

Flohmann proposed that the index of cells with sufficient driving power is semi-columnar, which, as they grow towards the channel, are changed in the form of shape-shifted cells and are removed from the form of columnar cells.. After the cleansing showers and acute steron, if present, chronic serobitis is treated in the following order: 1. Burning the wound with electricity. 2. Partial incision of the cervix. Pregnancy after treatment. Cervical cancer usually appears after years of chronic servicitis. Eradicating tissue infected with recurrent tumors is one of the ways to prevent cancer. Any chronic disease of the cervix should be considered for the possibility of cervical cancer, and the spots necessary for cytology study after dissection or displacement. Cutting the patient's tissue should be removed. If the general result leads to the diagnosis of neck cancer Compassion is an urgent treatment.

Hemorrhoids entering the cervix(mucus

)With the chronic changes of amasi, it is possible to create hemorrhoids that enter the cervix.. Vaginal mucus discharge and bleeding are common symptoms. Most of the hemorrhoids can be separated from its location in the office. When the base of the hemorrhoid is located above and in the neck corridor, it is necessary to expand the neck and completely separate the hemorrhoid with the help of anesthetizing the patient. All the separated pieces have been subjected to less displacement changes. It should be sent for histological study.

Neck contraction

Neck contraction may be the origin of evolution(hereditary). Most of the time, the main causes of this hot discomfort are caused by burning, partial cutting,

cutting and cutting, cervical laceration ,

Obstruction of the cervical canal. Dryness after menopause leads to contractions and is often the cause. The closure is complete. In the latter case, pus may accumulate in the uterus. In postmenopausal women, cancer is one of the common causes of obstruction due to the accumulation of pus in the uterus. Many women suffering from cervical contracture show symptoms. It does not smell. Painful menstruation, irregular bleeding, discharge of white and sticky material from the hole.

Uterus and sterility can also be obtained. In the absence of neoplasm, repeating the dilation operation may be effective in repairing the contraction. Partial cutting is rarely used and usually in Hysterectomy is necessary in such cases or cases accompanied by other diseases..Accumulation of pus in the uterus requires dilation with the help of anesthetizing the patient and using suction.. study of stain or culture may be useful in determining the effective antibacterial agent.

Growing up(high growth)

The enlargement resulting from the extension of the internal part of the cervix sometimes occurs without causing an infection.. How does progress inside or outside cause discomfort if a hysterectomy Another treatment method, Rajur showed, is to use cutting method..

Remaining neck wounds

Neck wounds left after partial hysterectomy may cause harmless diseases that are discussed in this chapter.. For treatment and improvement .It is better to cut through the vagina.

Wounds of the uterus, endometriosis

Except in cases of pregnancy, myositis is the most important reason for the enlargement of the uterus.. Since they have the origin of muscle cells, therefore, they cannot be considered in the "fibrous" row. The related tissues are also a part of this rule. However, if the growth of such tissue is confirmed, it can be called fibromyoma or fibromyalgia. If the myometrium includes the glands of the endometrium, it is called adenomyoma or myometrium.

Black skin is seen. This disease is often diagnosed in patients between the ages of 30 and 45. It is given. Pregnancy may be the cause of fibromyalgia, but it does not play a role in their occurrence because this condition is found mostly in the uterus of women who have never given birth. After menstruation stops, new swelling is not created, and the existing swellings also regress, but they do not disappear completely.

A rapid increase in volume after menopause, the possibility of the existence of a lump, including .The large spindle cells have become stronger, and the swelling, which is harmless, gradually increases.

 Muscle swelling may be single, but usually it is in the form of a group, and their size varies between the microscopic size and the huge sizes of the body. In terms of special features, the small spherical swelling is capsule-like, which is exposed to the removal of the nucleus, and if their surface is cut, it has a ring-shaped appearance. Under the microscope, a bunch of smooth muscle cells can be seen scattered in different directions. The shape of the cells varies between round and polyhedral or spherical and depends on whether the stems are cut obliquely or longitudinally. Its kernels are inclined and its end is slightly round.

Secondary changes

The appearance of myositis is of any size, it can be amazing under. The effect of the following factors will change. stages and degrees of descent, in addition to transparency, bag, fat, Calcareous, infectious, depending on Ghanqaria or bone corruption, cell death and deterioration(meat), depending on Meat and slimming product. changes in the expansion of lymphatic vessels and swelling of the vein or skin accumulation .

location:

intramural between the smooth muscle of the uterus; submucosa, under the inner lining of the uterus, Subserous subperitoneum. The last two stages are often stemmed. Myositis may be physical, rule, neck, intra-joint or parasitic. The last name mentioned by the scholars of the disease. It has been diagnosed and is also called as vagus myositis..

Signs and symptoms

Signs and symptoms depend on the location and size of myometrium.. In many patients, the situation is such that they do not express any discomfort. Growth of submucosa from discomfort It is the most painful stage that causes discomfort to the inner lining of the uterus and bleeding starts.. Usually, at first, it occurs in the form of excessive bleeding. Then, the duration and amount of zinc blood may cause anemia and jaundice. Cervical myositis may lead to Vaginal bleeding and in some cases causes painful intercourse in women..When pressure is also accompanied by this discomfort, swelling of the bladder, rectum, ovaries. Nerves or other organs are violated. Infection, cell death and deterioration, and Ghanqaria or bone corruption, causing pain, fever, increasing the level of The presence of red cells and colorless cells is considered as the general rule of symptoms.. The complication of the operation on the vein to prevent bleeding was very painful and maybe that is the reason.. Abnormal childbirth due to the contraction of the birth canal muscle mass. be. Other possible discomforts related to pregnancy may include infertility, miscarriage, uterine displacement, abnormal fetal appearance and displacement, uterine laziness, postmenstrual bleeding, and abnormal uterine rotation. Pregnancy due to endometrial fibroids sometimes occurs. The pelvic girdle causes contraction.

Diagnosis

Accumulations of excess growth attached to the uterus may be mistaken for myositis.. Adhesions Growing up Uterus, maybe due to the harmless progression of the endometrium into the uterus or efective rotation. be merciful. Despite the fact that the uterus may not be as large as it should be, it is likely to cause the growth of an uncomfortable submucosal fibroid, which is caused by a surgical tool or Hysterography can be identified. In cases of infertility, the possibility of myositis is more.

Treatment

Small swellings that do not cause discomfort do not need treatment.. Often, during normal examinations, this group of tumors is encountered. In order to cover it from the patient's point of view, he should be convinced that such swellings are harmless, and he should confirm that at least once every six months for an examination. Consult your doctor. There are some of these small swellings that are excluded from this rule of "being symptomless, not needing treatment", including cervical myositis. Separating them through.

The vagina is much easier. 12-week gestational age without swelling-related symptoms. The uterine muscle needs surgical treatment due to the possibility of secondary discomfort.. In young patients, discomforts related to uterine bleeding accompanied by myometriosis may be treated with estrogen and other hormones, but if the result is not satisfactory, the effort to find myometriosis under the mucous layer should not be made.

If the existing symptoms require surgery, gynecology specialists should consider the following points in the patient.

The patient's age, pregnancy and the like, her inclination to pregnancy, the location, size, position and number of muscle swellings and the general condition of the patient in addition to discomfort-producing factors. Scraping the tumors from the uterine wall may stop the uterine bleeding and cause cancer to enter the uterine lining in some patients. In any case, if the uterine cavity is sufficiently complicated, the treatment with the Trasch method is not considered sufficient. In this case, study of lexology is also emphasized be.

Tumors are removed surgically in necessary cases, and this is in a case where The patient needs definitive treatment and the uterus must be taken care of.. Some of the sterility as well They may be treated in the following order, provided that the person is sure that all factors of infertility have been taken into consideration.. Swellings without signs and symptoms during surgery related to If the pelvic cavity has developed, it can be usually treated in the same order.. usually due to the muscularity of the uterus in the caesarean section, the myometrium is removed by the method It seems like a normal problem. Swelling that is possible in some way during the birth of a baby. It should close the related blood vessels and stop the blood.

The more obvious the muscle swelling is, the easier it is to remove it. Before the hysterectomy, the patient and her husband should be invited to discuss the intended operation and the main operation of the proposed uterus. It should be explained to them in a clear way, and in particular, more attention should be paid to the operation of the rule. The topic should be analyzed as it should be.. At this point, activity should be discussed Ovaries should be presented and it should be explained that the ovaries are in the form of glands that secrete. They have internal organs that remain active even after removing the uterus, and in this case, as a result, they remain in the same state unless the requirements for rooting them out.. A patient who has to undergo hysterectomy and bilateral salpingoectomy. It is interesting to explain some points about the activities of "female hormones" and their production by the Rochliov gland. In any case, before starting the operation, a necessary decision should be made about the surgical procedure, and in general, a person should not perform an incomplete surgery and remove the body of the uterus but leave the cervix.

Fortunately, modern anesthesia, advances in surgical techniques and tools, and the existence of antimicrobial agents, etc., make complete hysterectomy more than the changes related to the above. The cervix faces fewer risks. In case of urea trosystocel, Rectocele, enterocele, or real stretch or uterine stretch diagram and uterine swelling reduction to the size of the twelfth week of pregnancy, vaginal hysterectomy will not be necessary. the condition that pelvic swelling or endometrial diseases are not observed. Ovarian cysts, Adjunctive growths, noticeable tumors in the lower bladder, usually in the near contralateral judgment. It is a vaginal treatment. Radiation treatment of myositis is mostly for those patients who need surgery.

It was not possible, but due to bleeding, he could not guarantee its preservation and needs treatment. be. With the passage of time, this group of patients decreased to such an extent that their number has reached zero. Dr. RJ Krusen points out that radium treatment by some researchers .It has been inadvertently criticized because it was thought that the presence of a soft tissue for radiation may cause endometrial cancer in the later years of life.. In general, it is an undeniable fact that the effect of radiation is primarily due to the act of ovulating. be. For this reason, gynecology specialists are advised to perform surgery to save the ovaries, unless there is a sufficient reason to uproot them, or the patient cannot tolerate surgery. Urinary tract cancerous tumors grow in the absence or presence of endometriosis, but the presence of endometriosis in the person's uterus leads to the danger that .It does not lead to a higher than average risk of colon cancer.

Uterine hemorrhoid

It is called mucous membrane. These hemorrhoids related to amas of the mucous membrane are called. These hemorrhoids should be compared with mucous hemorrhoid which is the cause of most of the ups and downs from the cervix. He discussed the hemorrhoids consisting of the undeveloped and defective endometrium and the group consisting of the active endometrium and examined their cleaning problems under the microscope.

Dangerous corruption of hemorrhoids without danger happens less often, but maybe there is a lot of danger and damage. Depending on the hemorrhoids, the inner membrane of the uterus with a uterine cavity filled with piles is called hemorrhoids.. Hemorrhoids can be small or multiple. Let it be big enough to fill the uterine cavity. The stem of the hemorrhoids can be short or long.

 It should be tall because the reason for the prolapse of the hemorrhoids is from the neck passage to the vagina and sometimes from the genital area.. Clinical symptoms are less common than small hemorrhoids,. A bruise is a result of an injury as a result of a sexual wound.. In some cases of patients suffering from zinc blood, there is between two periods. Cochlear hemorrhoids, glandular myometrial tumor, is definitely a type of endometrial tumor, cochlear hemorrhoids related to the pair of fetuses, abortion, defective fetus or Residual development depends on the fetal pair, which maintains its connection to the uterus even after birth, even after months or years.. A knowledgeable person will find on microscopic examination the corruption of the furuncle or hair growth of furuncle or outer membrane of fetus surrounded by blood clots..

Treatment

If the hemorrhoid is single, it is usually easy to remove.. The common method of neck dilatation and It is uterine discharge. A Randall's stone forceps or sponge forceps should be used for Hemorrhoid probe should be used because it may not be accessible with conventional surgical instruments.. It is clear that the act of shaving must be complete because there may be other dangerous factors. It should also be present in the uterine cavity. In the case of a specific muscle abscess accompanied by bleeding due to an infectious hemorrhoid that protrudes from the cervix, the best way to isolate the hemorrhoid and treat the infection before the root is to remove the uterus.

Arteriosclerosis and cysts

Lymphatic tumor is a rare uterine wound, and harmless vascular tumor is even rarer.. Pedowitz and his colleagues on the issue of uterine fibroids and varicose veins and sacs and Spindle-like cell tumors and muscle network were carefully studied.. Gartner's duct bags, a similar discussion is detailed in the third chapter..

Uterine cancer

There are three types of neoplasms that may originate from the uterus.

 Derived from the skin of the mucous membrane, it has a trophoblastic origin and in the season13 will be discussed.

Cervical cancer

Cervical cancer is the most common cancer in women after breast cancer, and it is one of the most common cancers of the reproductive system.. Previously, it was reported that the incidence of this cancer was eight times higher than that of endometrial cancer. Recently, it is believed that the incidence rate is four times that of endometrial cancer, and in some cervical cancer patients, it is less.

 t was endometrial cancer. It has been estimated that 2% of women over the age of 40 will suffer from neck cancer. Almost the majority of these cancers are of the type of cells with a similar shape, the remaining 5% are in the form of glandular cancer.

Cervical cancer-like cells

Almost the majority of cancer-like cells originate from the columnar junction, a region that affects the cells of the mucous membrane from both sides. Basal cells appear to be precursors of cancerous tumor changes.. Rare cases of cancerous cells have been diagnosed in young girls.. However, the average age for the diagnosis of cancer is around 36 years old. In comparison with the excessive proliferation of basic cells, cancer tumors are observed in the microscopic examination of defects in the layering of the cervical mucous membrane and its placement by cancer cells.

 It is impossible to attack through the basic layers. Its origin may be from several bases. It should be the neck or mucosal membrane on the side of the vagina. When it is seen in the neck gland and cells, as explained by Flohmann, the diagnosis is often made from the histological point of view of invasive carcinoma.

A patient who Suffering from aggressive cancer and will remain in the variable period for the next ten years.. When the vaginal part of the cervix is studied in this period of the disease, it is usually considered harmless. In fact, approximately one fifth of patients who show cancer. They have a completely normal cervix. The diagnosis of other patients consists of neck and corruption. It is gradual or reversible. If symptoms and signs appear, it will be related to the neck. The average age of the patients for the aggressive form of the tumor is around 47 years old, and this fact leads us to think that in some cases, cancer has been hidden for about ten years before the appearance of the tumor. The large wounds that appear may be of a type where the place of their impact is in the form of a lump and sometimes in the form of a cabbage flower growth, which is called the form of external growth of cancer. In other patients, the growth is generally aggressive and internal growth, and the focus is a region of stiffness and tearing in will come.

The cervix may be dilated. After the presence of invasive cancer has changed from months to years, the patient may have discharge of watery substances and nasal discharge, especially if contact with the cervix is made during intercourse..

It is necessary to emphasize that when you see these symptoms, you should know that the cancer is in more advanced stages. When the cancer spreads to the tissues and extends from there to the broad ligament and the upper vagina, tenderness and pain may occur. This cancerous growth can be pulled up and into the body of the uterus. This is spread before and after by procedures.

A sheet in the shape of the bladder and rectum may be limited.. In the initial stages of the invasion, it is also possible for blackness to penetrate. Attack on blood vessels .It is a sign of a bad disease that follows. It is possible to differentiate venous from lymphatic. It is necessary to have hot stretchy fabrics. The invasion of the lymphatics leads to a relatively early occurrence and displacement of the external serine inflammation, the obstructed total inflammation and the internalized serine inflammation, and the common serine may be achieved gradually. Amas may be observed in cases where another Amas cannot be seen outside the cervix depending on the histology, and this situation.

It will lead to the dependence of the lymphatic vessel. It bypasses the urinary tract by stretching or lymphatic extension. Obstruction of the urinary tract is due to the progressive expansion of the pelvis and renal pelvis, kidney and pelvic edema. The stretching of the side wall of the pelvis and the stiffness and strengthening that follows may be accompanied by an increase in the pelvis and back. When the wall of the bladder is invaded by the disease, the first sign of the need for cystoscopy is the presence of abscesses filled with blood.

Wounds and presence of blood in the urine are secondary symptoms that appear later. Similar effects may also appear in the rectum. With the corruption of the tissue, a new cancer can be created. Amas Hai Cervical carcinoma is usually accompanied by some degrees of swelling of the bee tissue and It is possible that endometrial cysts and fallopian tube cysts also follow.. Many times, the infection's hardness and fibrousness when touched cannot be identified and cleaned from the contraction of a cancerous tumor, and its growth may be the cause of the obstruction of the uterine neck and cause the accumulation of pus in the uterus.. (This condition is more likely to be accompanied by a cancerous tumor in the shape of a cervical gland).

Failure is related to unhappiness. Transmission of different diseases has been reported in 25 to 45 percent of autopsy cases. Sequence order It has been recorded in liver, bone, spleen, intestine and stomach, brain and skin..As mentioned earlier, the patient may suffer from vaginal pain and bleeding.. With the gradual analysis and corruption of a certain amount of cervical or vaginal veins, this bleeding. It seems more. more advanced stages of cancer with stimulation of the pelvic nerves or nerves that The dark medulla creates a lot of pain to transmit the remaining disease.

Almost the majority Patients who died from cervical cancer, the cause of their death is bloody urine due to ureteral obstruction and damage to kidney function.. Intestinal obstruction is possible due to Transmission of the disease. Cervical cancer stage is extremely important and is related to histological stages to some extent (Browder), but it is more related to the classification of the disease, which will be discussed in the next chapter. It is enough to say that according to a report from California, only 15% of patients diagnosed with uterine cancer histopathologically survived only five years. are.

Glandular carcinoma of the cervix

Carcinoma of the cervix may appear as a sore from the cervix, but it is rarely seen in this way.. When this disease was recognized, the extension and scope of its invasion was bigger and more than the cancerous tumors of the cell shape, even in the case of Patients who have been regularly under medical examination. The tendency of lymphatic development of this type of histology. It is similar to a cancerous cell. The origin of about half of the cancerous tumor of the gland .The shape inside the cervix is from the inner membrane of the uterus.

Scientific motivation

Despite the fact that the primary cause of the dangerous factors for the cervix is not evident, but the factors. It is associated with the occurrence of cancer. Women with chronic service, longer intercourse years and More pregnancy, they suffer from dangerous factors for entering the cervix, and on the other hand, cervical cancer in single and single women is almost zero, and with the necessary treatment . It rarely happens. Jewish women have fewer risk factors than non-Jewish women. They go inside the cervix. Poor and underprivileged women are affected by this disease.

Diagnosis

It is highly recommended that all cervical cancer foci be diagnosed in the early stages of the disease and this will not be possible except with regular pelvic examination, which should be performed at least once in women who show symptoms of the disease and get married. They are married, it will be done. If this disease is accompanied by another disease, more frequency should be used in the examination. slave. In order to diagnose the symptoms in the early stages, cytology studies should be used more and more often. It is worth noting that 20% of cancerous tumors in Zamha Bezreg are from. It does not show blood. If large wounds are a sign of cancer, biopsy samples should be taken. It was removed and used for cytology stain.

When reversals, gradual deterioration, and pockets appear harmless, spot testing should confirm the issue of harmlessness before heating the tissue in question. If the result of the pap smear is classified as 3, 4 or 5, the pap smear should be removed again and a biopsy should be performed. To take the necessary stain for biopsy, Schiller's stain may be useful. When added to gram or tolugol iodine solution. The skin of the natural mucous membrane has a reddish-brown color due to the presence of glycogen, while the tissues suffering from benign or neoplastic diseases do not acquire this color.. The suspicious area can be biopsied. In order to make sure that the area is not invaded by another cancer, it is necessary to remove a tissue cone from the cervix so that it can be He moved all the centers of the considered neoplasm. Then different parts of it. The presence of a cancerous or invasive tumor is diagnosed..

Clinical classification of cervical cancer

The international classification of cervical cancer grades is as follows.:

stage cancer foci in the center:

This stage is called a cancerous tumor that has not yet invaded other tissues. It is also called similar. At this stage, the cancer is limited exclusively to the cervix. The cancerous tumor is spread from the cervix to the other side, but it has not yet reached the pelvic wall. It is. Cancer tumors include the vagina as well, except for the lower third. Cancer has reached the pelvic wallIn the examination of the rectum, there is no cancer-free space between the tumor and the pelvic wall. Cancer center including the lower third of the vagina .It will also happen. Cancer tumors include the bladder, the rectum, or both, or to the extent that was mentioned before. By touching it, you can determine the degree of cancer progression. As mentioned above, the gradual deterioration of the active infection of the fibrous structures that follows the infection may be mistaken for a cancerous tumor and the presence of an internal membrane tumor.

Uterus, ovarian swellings or uterine fibroids may cause more confusion and confusion.. Lymphatic swellings carrying pelvic tumors are usually not felt and can be found only in cases of accurate histological examination after surgery. Classification under selection after Surgery shows the relationship between the manifestations as a relationship with clinical cancer grading.: stage1:The connection of events15%. stage2: The connection of events%25 stage3 and 4: The connection of events30%

(estimated after abdominal distension): correlation of outcomes after radiation42% (estimated after tearing the stomach).

Treatment

If we want the treatment to be effective, all dangerous tissues must be removed from the body or destroyed. turn around. If such an action is not possible, the treatment will only have an analgesic aspect. As before We have been reminded that when discussing cancer in the center, accurate and correct diagnosis is extremely important, and this operation requires sufficient tissue cutting and histological examination.. If the patient is suffering from young cancerous tumors and wants to get pregnant, cold and deep conic tissue cutting should be done and the patient should be examined once every six months and then allowed to get pregnant. If pregnancy is not desired by the patient, the uterus should be separated from the body through the vagina or abdomen. It is not unusual for the side wall of the vagina to be separated as well, especially if the color is yellow in normal condition.

Don't hold back. When the cancerous tumor has spread to the free connective tissue and the smooth muscle layer between the two layers and the bond, it is extremely important to determine the position of the uterus with the help of pyelography. Whether it is surgical treatment or radiology, compensation of anemia and clearing of infection in order to obtain a complete result and It is necessary to avoid future inconveniences. Almost most cervical cancer today is treated with radiation.. in some Centers in the case of some patients selected from surgery for primary treatment .

Radiation therapy

The radiation sources used are radium, cobalt.60, gold. It is usually provided. This radiation is the unit of absorption of food medicine and also as. The scale of energy created by ionizing radiation in each unit is the accumulation of factors that are under radiation and is equal to It is 100 raj per gram. Ionizing radiation causes chemical changes between cells with H2O for complex proteins. The histological evidence of these chemical changes are small pits in the cell protoplasm, chromatin changes, and membrane separation.

They are cellular, tissue damage or bone necrosis, an increase in lymphocytes and plasma cells..The necessary principles for the basis of radiation therapy, here as everywhere else in the body, its abundant effect is on the tissue with abnormal growth and tumor-like growth as opposed to the normal tissue.. Since the cervix is accessible for direct treatment, radiation can be placed between the cervical canal and the uterus. This method is usually done with the help of radium or cobalt tubes, which are done with the help of a rubber in a row or a plastic vessel called row and back to back

. The use of the cervix at the entrance of the vagina is done with the help of colpousitis. The size of the uterus, the cervix, and the size of the vagina, as well as the size of the growth, dominates the radiation distance. It is usually intended that all but the gamma rays be sent out, and to measure the beam of radiation, the radium salt can be filtered with a metal, usually platinum or copper, of the beam. It measured the emitted radiation. Knowing this measurement along with the design of the same curvatures as the Phantom Lake allows this.

He predicted the beam of radiant light that reaches every point.. As it can be seen from the above discussion, the radiation means must be done exclusively by a doctor who has enough knowledge and experience in the work of radiation medicine, because each patient is tested with another patient. There is a huge difference. It is also necessary for this doctor to be knowledgeable about the science of the female reproductive system in order to avoid the discomforts of tissue corruption along with endometriosis or ovarian neoplasms. In the same way, he should also consider the possibility of intestinal adhesion around the uterus or coccyx. Evaluate.

The use of radiation takes place by dilating and opening the cervix and sending radiation from inside the uterus. Vagina in order to avoid exposure to radiation, to keep the bladder and rectum away from the ulcer. It is full of gauss. The important point is that the bladder should be kept empty with the help of a special tube, and the rectum and the bladder should also be emptied before and kept in this state during the entire period that the patient is under radiation. The methods and different ways of using radium are not mentioned here. In addition to the radiation that is directly given to the tumor through the skin, it also aims to deliver radiation to the pelvic lymph nodes and enough radiation to destroy the swollen tissue to minimize death. Radiation is used to block lymphatics and cancer cells.. When there is an infection or dilation of the cervix, it is possible to use external radiation or radiation through the vagina before using direct radiation on the cervix. This action prevents the patient from getting infected.

It shows and causes the wounds to shrink and shrink for better accommodation, and it becomes colpocytized.. 250

kilovolt machines are usually used. The radiation trap can also be used in the form of a radium bomb or recently in the form of a cobalt bomb. Cobalt bombs with strong pressure X-ray machines have more light penetration power.. Therefore, skin damage is very important He doesn't come. Although large amounts of light can be delivered to the skin without causing damage. In addition, there is a risk of damage to the skin of the intestinal system and the possibility of injury and perforation. And that is why the use of high pressure radiation is limited.. It has been tried to use radioactive cobalt threads or by using the device.

Among the advantages of radiation therapy in the treatment of cancer tumors, while infection is limited, the number of deaths is much less. In the absence of referral to surgeons, more patients can be treated under the supervision of qualified doctors who are knowledgeable about radiation therapy. This group of patients ,They occupy less space in hospitals and need less nursing, which is approximately. It is the exact opposite of the situation when patients undergo surgery.. They have also faced special damages in radiation therapy. During the use of radiation, both externally and internally, nausea and vomiting occur.

These conditions can usually be eliminated by using anti-nausea and vomiting medicine. Side effects related to fever may be uncomfortable or may be due to radiation in any selenium. Reactions related to fever due to exacerbation of existing infection are usually curable with antibacterial agents; But sometimes it is necessary to stop the radiation treatment that is given directly to the cervix. Movement related to the right intestine along with diarrhea and straining or twisting has also been seen more or less. If the pain is beyond the tolerance of the rectum, the abscess of the rectum is fully visible and a wound or perforation is possible. It has happened. As predicted, black vomit or black vomit was seen along with the wound. Bladder is more resistant to radiation, however, frequency of urine or pressurized urine is often seen. The need to use a special towel for drying causes an increase in the possibility of bladder inflammation.

The radiation that goes into the bladder or the rectum is measured, and also reviewing the irradiated area with the help of X-ray film can prevent damage to the bladder and rectum.. When radiation is used to destroy the cancer, the secretory function of the ovaries is limited so that menstruation stops. Failure to recognize the occurrence of disease transmission can be attributed to the overuse of radiation therapy.

Surgical treatment

Considering that surgical treatment for uterine cancer is accepted by the experts. There is a difference of opinion in applying the same treatment for other stages.. When the cancerous tumor is limited to the cervix and the adjacent organs of the vagina and the free tissue spreads between the two layers of the connective tissue, complete excision is possible.

This operation is possible by approaching the vagina according to Shawta's principles, because of the complete separation of the uterus and the free tissue between the two layers of the wide ligament after the complete equipment of the urinary organs, but this method cannot be effective in cutting the lymph nodes. . By approaching through the abdomen, the uterus and free tissue between the two layers of connective tissue can be separated next to the adjacent organs of the vagina, and they can also separate the pelvic lymph nodes from the veins and arteries of the pelvis. When the swelling attacks the bladder, a cystectomy can be performed and the ureter can be transferred to a pouch formed by the long intestine. In the same way, when the rectum is attacked, the rectum can be separated and a colostomy can be formed.

With the advancement of the science of anesthesia, more blood in hospitals, the use of antibacterial agents, and knowledge of the science of electrolyte balance, more frequent surgeries can be performed with less death. In fact, today, the way of tearing the abdomen with less than 10% mortality is acceptable. Mortality in surgery with the method Shavata or Vertim from1% does not violate. The advantages of surgical excision of cancer in the cervix is that the isolated swelling can be well used in the laboratory. With surgical incision, not only accurate diagnosis is possible, but also the period of discomfort and the course of the disease can be predicted with more accuracy. Again, not alone

The gradual leakage of the tissue extension between the two layers of the wide coverage graft can be determined more accurately, but the range of other diseases such as intestinal adhesions or other uterine or ovarian tumors can be determined.. Surgical treatment in young women may cause tissue release.

Ovarian cancer because it has been seen less often that cervical cancer spreads to the ovaries as well.. By tearing open the abdomen, it causes the return of urinary flow, and with necessary drying, the renal function is improved. Another advantage of surgical incision is that it causes the removal of the swollen tissue, which is not necessary with radiation treatment and in some cases it also causes tissue separation. As a result of the radiation, he suffered from infection and gonorrhea.. The main disadvantage of surgical treatment is the need for the surgeon's skill.

The death rate is much higher due to the radiation method, careful nursing after surgery, and long-term hospitalization of the patient after surgery. There is often a need for blood transfusion, and the threat of bleeding during surgery and after surgery should also be considered. Hematoma and lymph pooling also occur in the pelvis.

The more advanced Kanjanj Ilaus has been seen a lot. You should expect the bladder to be loose, which is accompanied by prolonged dissection and dissection. The swollen area should be removed, and this situation requires long-term drying of the bladder with the help of a surgical needle. If you cannot remove the swollen area in time Cancer has also been cut, it is possible that the scope of the swelling will increase.. The biggest problem of Shawuta and Vertim surgeries and dissection and excision of the nasolacrimal gland.

Low pressure rectal surgery has been seen many times in urinary retention.. As it was said before, the necessary surgery, i.e. shortening of the vagina, will of course disappear with the method of tearing the vagina, and sexual intercourse will be impossible. Inconveniences related to bowel retention Long or colostomy should not be ignored in cases of abdominal pain..

A set of treatment methods

Although the spread of nodular discomfort cannot be determined without having a surgical sample, it has been tried to make it possible to treat it.. Efforts in cytology, morphology, etc The changes related to the general study of the cell are in the radiation.. When Amasi Adjacent, intestinal adhesions or myositis may also be noticeable along with the treatment. Surgery is considered appropriate to prevent radiation disorders and tissue damage.. From Serious proponents of Brunswick surgery can be mentioned, who recommend surgery for all patients.. Others, like Meigs and Parsons, suggest that surgical treatment is necessary.

They suggest to limit the cutting of the uterus and the free tissue between the two layers of the wide graft as much as possible in the case of aggressive wounds that are in the initial stages and are not more than one centimeter in diameter, because there is a possibility of the presence of nodules. It is very insignificant in this category. Some believe that a local cut is used so that the radiation in the treatment is ineffective. Here The problem is that when should the surgery be done? When the defect is Cytotoxicity has been evaluated in such cases, the result is that this action is advanced. Sensation when touching the cancerous tumor of the cervix shows it only in the case of a few patients. DH.

Subsequent examinations

All patients who have been treated for neck cancer in one way or another should be closely examined for a period of one year and after that every six months. examined precisely. To be sure of the effect of the treatment, the first examinations are necessary and even mandatory. After the inflammatory treatment to separate any adhesions that may be in the vagina and to guide the patient in vaginal hygiene, initial examinations are among the necessities.. The next steps for these patients may include cytology studies and biopsy. What a wound It should be biopsied.

It is necessary to evaluate the urinary tract carefully, this Evaluation should not only include chemical or microscopic analysis of urea, but also tallow. respectively, displaced lesions of the vertebral column may be seen on X-ray films.. After a period of time, it is possible to create a bone tumor after radiation. Therefore, this condition should be able to be cleaned with the corruption of the recurrent cancer tissue. If the patient can stay healthy for five consecutive years, it can be said that his disease has been controlled. But in the case of other types of cancer, other parts of the body, especially the vagina and rectum, should be carefully examined.

Predicting the period of unhappiness

Convergence in predicting the period of discomfort after radiation therapy for cervical cancer. With primary surgical treatment, the five-year survival rate is 82% for first-stage wounds and 62% for second-stage wounds. between patients with first degree lesions with positive survival outcomes 40 to 50%; Patients with second-degree wounds with a survival rate between 10 and 20% and patients with urethritis, bladder and vagina10% seen It is. As you mentioned before, the stomach tearing method has approximately 10% death rate. In terms of the survival of patients who have been introduced for treatment with the abdominal incision method, the survival rate of 30% has also been reported. like when the stomach hurts.

Cervical cancer during pregnancy

Diagnosis of visceral cancer during pregnancy is usually made after confirming the presence of abnormal cells in cytology stains.. Drilling biopsies Multiple or separation of cone-shaped tissue can be done without miscarriage.. If it is known that the wound is in the intestines, the pregnancy can continue. It is worth noting that the serious stages of the cancerous tumors observed in the intestines during pregnancy did not disappear after the pregnancy. In any case, the lack of knowledge in the pathology of the cellular changes in the cervix during pregnancy can easily be mistaken for a cancerous tumor in the viscera.

As aggressive cancer was observed in the early stages of pregnancy, the smallest damage should not be done to the pregnancy; Cancer should be treated as if the patient is not pregnant, except that if radiation is needed, hysterectomy is necessary. Some suggest that due to the increase in the similarity of the development of neoplasm with the expiration of pregnancy, surgical treatment is better than radiation therapy in cervical cancer seen in early pregnancy. When you It is not possible to diagnose the disease before the end of pregnancy, the pregnancy must continue. and you should try to treat it only after the situation..

Care of suspected cervical cancer patients

Since cervical cancer patients are dying because of this disease, it is necessary to take proper care of them.. One of the main issues of reduction. The pain is sick. In the initial stages of the patient, the factors of the defects of the pain can be identified. The solution is to cut the nerve connection of this area with the help of alcohol injections in the network and areas of the cobweb or by cordotomy; However, these methods are rarely used. The psychological treatment of the doctor's father greatly increases the patient's hidden pain .

Glandular carcinoma of the endometrium

Endometrial cancer is the second most common cancer compared to reproductive organs.. With increasing longevity, more women reach an age where the pressure of this disease is usually at its maximum. arrived. In this order, the incidence of this disease, such as cervical cancer, increases.

Scientific motivation

Despite the fact that young women also suffer from this disease, the problems are less, the patient is less than It has been observed for 40 years. Two thirds of the patients were between the ages of 50 and 70. The interesting thing here is that the patients suffering from this disease are obese or suffering from high blood pressure and some. They have also suffered from diabetes.

Patients suffering from excessive growth of the endometrium have prolonged menstruation. Patients suffering from estrogen-producing ovarian tumors are more prone to suffering from this disease, which leads us to the fact that continuous and long-term stimulation of the body's estrogenic period will make the body more resistant to neoplasms or excessive growth of endometrium.. Acute forms of cell proliferation related to the endometrium have been observed when external estrogens have been used for a long time. The occurrence of papillary cell proliferation or the appearance of an increase in glandular cancerous tumors depending on the endometrium in patients suffering from discomforts related to bleeding in menopause or near menopause and general diseases.

Stein's displeasure- Luntal brings us closer to the fact that seepage plays a major role. In the development of this disease. Acquiring the fact that almost the majority of patients are not affected by this disease until one or two years after menopause and that many patients have been given multiple external estrogens for a long time without showing any progress in growth is the same. that stimulation of external estrogens was given without showing growth progress is enough to prove that Estrogen stimulation is only one of the effective factors in this disease..

Natural history

As we said in the motivational discussion, endometrial glandular cancerous tumor is usually diagnosed after menopause and it is known to be a cancerous tumor.

The endometrium can be considered as a precursor of cancerous and glandular tumors.. tendency to It depends on the occurrence of hemorrhoids.. Bleeding against cervical cancer It will probably appear in the early stages. The elements resulting from the growth may contain a large amount of mucus.

The discharge from the neck is a mixture of blood and mucus. If there is a stage of narrowing of the cervical canal before growth, there is a possibility of a more complete obstruction of the neck. It happened that it leads to the accumulation of pus in the uterus.. The scope of growth is different. Recently, it has been reported that in certain groups, 50% of patients suffering from the early stages of endometrial adenocarcinoma from the point of view of histology.

They have been diagnosed and survived for five years without treatment.. On other occasions, myositis attacks have happened. It is possible for the disease to spread with the invasion of myositis in this area to reach the cervical lymphatics as well. Fortunately, lymphatic foot This disease is not diagnosed unless several related symptoms are seen for a while.. with formation Accumulation in the uterine cavity or with the invasion of myometrium, the uterus may be dilated.. Sometimes this Accumulation may cause neck enlargement.

The study on the blood taken from the abdominal artery shows that during the test, the tumor cells enter the blood circulation many times from the inner membrane of the uterus. However, there is almost no sufficient reason for the entry of these types of cells into the blood circulation. In this way, despite the fact that the tumor cell enters the blood circulation, it is known that the resistance .Host factors prevent the establishment and activity of these types of cells.. How is the inflation?

The lymphatics of the neck are attacked, it is possible that this swelling will spread to the vaginal lymphatics as well.. This way of spreading the disease, along with direct placement in the vaginal wall during surgery, can be an obvious reason for the spread of the disease after surgery. By cutting through the uterine wall, peritoneal radiation is possible. It will be done. in the same order, Amasi cells may open the way to the fallopian tube and reside in the ovary or peritoneal cavity. turn around. From the point of view of the spread of the disease, this disease first affects the liver, then the liver, the skin and The bone is stretched. Patients who die as a result of endometrial cancer probably had intestinal obstruction and invasion of the kidney and bladder. It has also been seen in some cases of urinary tract cancer, such as cervical cancer. Pain attacks the patient with frequent intensity And the patient usually loses weight at first and dies in this case..

Diagnosis

The most important symptom of endometrial cancer is uterine abdominal bleeding.. Before menopause, it may appear as an intramural; Sometimes excessive bleeding is also likely to occur. A patient suffering from postmenstrual bleeding should be suspected of this disease. It should be diagnosed, especially if there is no abnormal condition in the cervix.. Although There is a possibility that bleeding after menopause may be accompanied by genital or vaginal disorders, as well as mild and harmless conditions such as cervical hemorrhoids or related to the endometrium, or following the use of a condom.

A patient suffering from myositis and especially suffering from a mixed discharge of mucus and blood should be specially treated. Doubtful to be diagnosed with endometrial cancer. The uterus may be dilated will be. The characteristic features of the cervical canal related to a healthy and safe tool or biopsy-related. It is the inner membrane of the uterus. Cytology study on elements obtained from the cervix or vagina may lead to the identification of malignant cells in 50-75% of patients with endometrial cancer. but a negative result has no practical value. The use of fluorescent stains in the following elements Cytology studies are more accurate in the diagnosis of endometrial cancer, but if a person wants to take more indicative results in the diagnosis of cytology studies depending on the membrane.

It is inside the uterus. It is necessary that the elements to be tested are from the cavity of the internal membrane of the uterus. It is necessary that the elements to be tested are obtained from the cavity of the internal membrane of the uterus by washing or rubbing.. Our opinion is that when the uterine cavity of an unconscious patient is attacked, it is preferable to take a sample of the tissue in question than to study cytology.

Biopsy before referring the patient to the hospital accelerates the necessary treatment. In order to get more accurate results, surgical incision is necessary. In order to estimate the growth area, it is especially necessary to take samples from the following areas: (1) from the cervix, (2) from the mucosal branch of the neck, (3) from the lowest part of the uterus and (4) from the upper part of the uterine cavity. The hairs that have been removed from these areas may be able to determine the extent of the spread of the cancer. With this information, the necessary treatment can be determined. In recent years, significant progress has been made in the method of removing good and frozen parts with the help of cryostat. Histological diagnosis has become faster and more accurate. The histological grading of the obtained tissues can approximate the degree of invasion. as indicated by the prevalence and type of large lesions..

Degree I

The gland is visible with a minimum amount of stroma. Invasion is either non-existent or very partial. It is. Cells with strange shapes appear with the increase in the proliferation of mucous membranes.

Degree II

The glandular form is less common. 25 to 50% of the cells multiply indirectly. They remain, and the stroma attack is completely visible.

Degree III

Unidentifiable cells 75%   50 Eli. The glandular shape becomes infinitely

Degree IV

Specific glands are not formed. Solid sheets of dangerous cells are seen. Acanthomatous changes may be seen and are characterized by areas of scaly cells that appear to originate from the metaplasm. The appearance of these areas seems to be in anticipation of the results The disease is not very effective.

Clinical classification

Stage 0

There is no trace of invasion. An anesthesiologist cannot attribute this whole situation to belief. To know cancer tumors.

Stage I

The growth of the uterus is limited. Grade-1, hysterectomy can be performed. Grade-2 due to existence .A dangerous disease cannot be hysterectomy.

Stage II

The growth is out of the womb.

Radiation therapy treatment:

In using radiation and to treat the degree1 Glandular tumor in the shape of the inner membrane of the uterus, there are different opinions. Those who are in favor of radiation and full abdominal hysterectomy and bilateral salpingo-oophorectomy believe that more favorable results can be achieved, because the transmission of the disease in the vaginal wall after surgery has been seen less. In the same way, radiation therapy before surgery causes the destruction of cancer cells. and may be present in the lymphatics around the cervix.

Almost the majority Specialists prescribe radiation around the cervix and inside the cervix as well as the uterine cavity before surgery, which uses radioactive radium or cobalt.. A few people suggest that X-rays be used for this purpose. Illnesses that should not be. They undergo surgery, radiation is the best method as an effective treatment with good results..

When a hysterectomy is not performed, it is necessary that the cavity related to the inner membrane of the uterus is completely irradiated.. The method of using double radium and filling the cavity depending on the inner membrane of the uterus with radium vessels, which was tested in Stockholm, met with great success. To achieve cervical incision and also vaginal incisions.

It is necessary to use coconuts. Endometrial cancer may be seen in patients suffering from the enlargement of the uterus and the complication of the cavity related to the endometrium due to myometrium. (It has not yet been proven that myositis is the reason for the development of glandular cancerous tumors). Swollen muscle tissue is likely to present as discomfort after radiation..

Surgical treatment

For the reasons that have already been detailed, surgical incision should also include the cervix.. Important point. This is where the ovaries and tubes should be removed due to the possibility of disease transmission.. In fact, the uterus that has been removed and if the histological diagnosis has not been done before the surgery, the cavity connected to the inner membrane of the uterus in the same operating room should be carefully reviewed so as not to An ovary that has a swollen tissue should be left. Cutting the pelvic lymph nodes is very appropriate because when it grew, it was spread to the lower part of the uterus. They prescribe lymphatic because they believe that in the presence of such disease carriers, it is not possible to predict the course of the disease as it should.. Some suggest that big events should be separated from symptoms for the purpose of prediction, and also .It is also possible to determine the amount of external radiation required..

Chemical treatment

In the year In 1961, it was reported that a type of combined progestin-17a hydroxy-progesterone-17-N-caprot is effective in patients with endometrial adenocarcinoma. It has been. In order to use this element as much as possible, 1.250 mg per week in. The muscle is injected. In almost the majority of patients, symptoms of improvement are observed and also from pain. has been reduced and their appetite has increased. The best evidence of using this drug is Defects in the size of palpable wounds or visible radiological wounds are visible.. The histological changes are related to the change in the secretory tissue along with the return of the acanthomacus neoplasm areas. The use of this element is not a definitive treatment, but rather as a sedative with little effect. It is a treatment.

Predicting the period of unhappiness

In a large number of patients who have been treated with different methods, the result Patients can live for five years. 45% of patients suffering from wounds of the second group can survive for five years. Stage injuries II shows a 5-year survival rate of up to 22% in patients. In the categories, especially in the advanced stages, from the point of view of diagnosis, the five-year life expectancy is up to It was 86%. The presence of growth in the cervix or the narrow area of the cervix and the increase in the size of the uterus are two signs. It is obvious that there is an uneven course of the disease.

The meat product of the womb

Such rare growths can be from any of the uterine tissues, from layers such as myometrium, related tissues, blood vessels, myometrium or stroma related to the membrane. They start inside the womb. Grape cluster meat products, although very rare and flower-colored, appear almost exclusively in children.. Derham layer tumors are mostly in patients between 40 and 60 years old. It has been seen. Smooth swelling of the uterine lining, which is one of the most famous uterine linings, usually. It appears in old age and it is likely that it originates from old myositis..

Diagnosis

Uterine fibroids can be identified when the bleeding started during childhood and an accumulation between the vagina is palpable or when it protrudes from the vagina.. Lumpy swelling of layered tumors has been observed in the last years of life and may appear as the cause of abnormal bleeding accompanied by the formation of accumulation.

 Some of these inflations have been obtained by obtaining elements in the section when examining such cases. Any patient whose uterus has grown rapidly, especially if this expansion has taken place after the cessation of menstruation, should be suspected of being pregnant. In some cases, the accumulation is out of the cervix and until the tissue corruption and pus discharge starts, the patient is aware of the new condition. It doesn't feel like it.

It can be somewhat difficult to detect the progressive degeneration of the meatus in a myositis.. This situation is more suspicious than it happens because of the corruption of the fabric and the fusion of corruption. The texture may cause this doubt. The spread of lehmi product takes place with continuous continuity, with blood circulation or with the lymphatic channel. The lung is the best place for the transmission of this disease. After that, from the point of view of frequency, it will be affected .He named the capacity of the liver, intestine, spleen, kidney, bladder, stomach and brain..

Treatment

Irradiation has been effective in very few cases of grape cluster meat products, and it has not had a noticeable effect on other types of meat products.. The only hope for treatment is surgical cutting of the uterus Inflation is before it finds its way out. The rate of five-year risk up to 30% .It has been reported. Amas of the middle layer of the dermis are especially a sign of a very bad disease.

Stones of the uterine trumpet

As mentioned in the third chapter, Morkagni sacs are among the general accumulation sacs connected to the root and blade.. Uterine sphincter amas, nodular barzakhi, swelling consisting of the inner lining of the uterus and muscular tissue, internal amas of Zahdan may lead to accumulation .They should be non-neoplasmic. Primary uterine tube cancer is the rarest cancer. They are productive systems. Even less dangerous swellings have seen.

Harmless tumors

Teratoma and benign tumors of muscular origin related to the tube, according to the report.They create palpable and twisted accumulations.. Glandular abscesses, hemorrhoids Glandular-shaped, benign tumors of muscular origin usually have symptoms and evidence. and other diseases have been diagnosed during surgery.

Dangerous tumors

The primary meat product is so low that only less than fifty percent of it is reported..Transplanted carcinomas of the fallopian tube are seen more often than the primary endometrium.. Ovarian and endometrial cancers are likely to spread to the fallopian tubes.. At The times of intervention, ovaries, tubes and endometrium in the disease, the origin of the neoplasm cannot be determined.. Primary cancerous tumor of the fallopian tube includes 0.1 to 1% of all discomforts. The reproductive organs of women are dangerous.

Pathology

The primary diagnosis of tubal cancer is variable and may spread as a scaly growth from the root end of the tubule.. Rooted end may be paired and trumpeted. The uterus is distended from swelling and fluid. The surgeon often thinks that it is possible Hydrosalpinx or piosalpinx is present.. In fact, uterine fibroids can also be accompanied by the formation of neoplasm. The spread of this growth is often done by preparing the surface of the surface. He accepts. Three microscopic groups have been determined:

Group I

The growth has a growth in the tube and some areas of the mucous membrane skin and a small amount of cells. It is limited during direct division.

Group II

Invasion of muscular and glandular forms is observed..

Group III

Invasion of lymphatics, cells in the process of direct differentiation, and solid sheets of cancer cells. It is found.

Diagnosis

Diagnosis is rarely needed before surgery.. Pelvic congestion before surgery. it is necessary that dangerous cells are seen in vaginal smears and there is no trace of neoplasm of the neck or related to the inner membrane of the uterus.. This situation has been used as a basic guide to correct diagnosis before surgery. When a uterine bleeding continues, especially when a neoplasm is not seen at the time of surgery, the possibility of tubal cancer is increased. Watery discharge following the temporary relief of abdominal pain as a symptom of Shippur's disease .It is a womb. When this problem is observed after the cessation of menstruation, it may be the cause.

Tubular cancer.

Treatment

Salpingo- Bilateral oophorectomy and hysterectomy should be performed. Except for grade I lesions that are limited to the fallopian tube, external radiation should be sampled by incision.

Forecasting the spread of the disease

in approx5 to 10% of the patients who have been treated for tubular cancer have achieved a 5-year survival. The best local results are found to be the end away from the center of the tube by AMAS.

A blocked fallopian tube and a degree wound I should be separated.

Amas of the inner lining of the uterus

in the year1921 Sampson draws the attention of scholars to a microscopic society of the endometrium of the uterus. And it has been seen there and in different places around the pelvic cavity to attract. in the womb Differentiation of the muscle content is called adenomyoma.. The external types of the uterus are sometimes called "external cysts". It is likely to form a sac containing elements that look like chocolate. In addition to the uterus and ovaries, possible sites include uterine joints (uterine, rectal, wide, and round); pelvic peritoneum that covers the uterus, fallopian tube, rectum, crescent, or bladder; appendix or appendix;

cervical spine. uterus, the effect of cutting the abdominal walls and caesarean section, hernia sacs, end of tube, umbilical cord, vulva, bladder, urine and Lymphatic gland. There are six of these discomforts under the armpit and shoulder.

Scientific motivation

Three important theories about the etiology of endometrial cancer are as follows.: Tubular restoration of the tissue of the inner lining of the uterus during menstruation with its subsequent placement and .Growth was proposed by Sampson. Without a doubt, this theory cannot cover all cases Explain the inflammation of the endometrium or the arrangement of the muscles in the uterus in general.. Some of the recent cases may be directly caused by the invasion.. The theory of metaplasm of the abdominal cavity or related to the abdominal cavity is based on the fact that The mucosal path of almost all areas of the Müllerian canal and also the mucous membrane skin.

The lining that covers the ovaries, and the pelvic peritoneum originate from this tissue.. Some of the parts that are less likely to change in the later years of life have the power to change, and this happens when other driving forces take over. They have that effect. Halban's opinion regarding the fact that the tumor of the endometrium can be explained in the context of the transmission of lymphatic disease or blood production has found many supporters. Javert's research proves that the endometrium can be harmless to the pelvic lymph nodes. and it may spread to the blood circulation.

Navak state that: "As far as we know, despite finding endometrium in pelvic lymph nodes, so far no one has been able to detect the clinical presence of pelvic endometrial tumor." Explain". Thelind and Scott proved that the endometrium peeling from the uterus during menstruation of a monkey can be implanted and grown on its peritoneum.. Meigs found that endometriosis was definitely a disease of private patients, and the intensity and weakness related between the patients and the patients of special care remain. He also suggests that the delay in marriage and the delay in having children in the economic and upper classes of the society may have motivational causes.

He points out that a small number of pregnancies in the patient group Private may also be a factor in the sentence. We are of the opinion with Stuart Taylor that the demand. There are more private patients for relief and relief of symptoms, and many more. Endometrial tumors have been diagnosed in the incision of the uterine walls.. He will He says "A patient in a private room with the same symptoms before surgery is often mistakenly and cautiously. They are treated through ovarian cysts and uterine tubes.".

Pathology

Internal and external membrane abscess sometimes in patients18 to 25 years old. However, almost the majority of people suffering from this disease are over 30 years old. Muscle spasms O-shaped gland has been seen in older patients(After 35 years old.) The course of this disease .It is different according to the progress or regression of symptoms and external investigations.. The main microscopic characteristics of the displacement of the endometrial gland, the stroma related to the endometrial membrane, the microbial cells of the hemispherical mucous membrane filled with hemosiderin; Large probes vary from a brownish-black solitary spot to densely attached pelvic organs.

It is. Dense lymphatic tissue develops in the reservoir of thick blood. The inner membrane of the displaced uterus gradually makes its way to the leakage and from there it goes to the abdominal wall where it often sticks to it. One of the most famous type of endometrial tumor of the ovarian sac is related to the inner membrane.

It is the uterus that all or some of its path is defined by endometrium-like tissue.. This tissue, which is under the influence of hormones, cannot function because the inner membrane of the uterus is surrounded from all sides and its blood supply is also done in an unnatural way. Bleeding inside the sac sometimes happens during menstruation, which results in the enlargement of the sac. Due to factors, it becomes dark and chocolate color. Gathering the contents of advanced tissue growth Depending on the inner lining of the uterus, or both, it may be the cause of the initial formation of the sac wall and the gradual penetration and finally resulting in the cultivation and dense adhesions of the patient's ovaries to the adjacent organs. When the inner membrane of the uterus is stretched to the pelvis, the pelvic cavity is frozen in this layer.

It is called because internal organs are motionless when touched.. Uterine endometriosis may exist without an external focus of the endometrium and appear scattered or limited. In the first case, it may cover the entire body of the uterus and become the cause of the diffuse thickening of the uterine wall. Although this gland, which is surrounded by the stroma related to the endometrium, may sometimes be activated by a sac-shaped space filled with stored menstrual blood, the tissue similar to the endometrium is often incomplete and inactive. It is correct that its origin is from the main part of the membrane.It should be inside the uterus, which does not interfere with the physiological changes resulting from the menstrual period.. Stromal endometriosis is a condition in which they believe that only the stroma attached to the endometrium attacks the endometrium. Navak and Navak Alirgham lack of glandular elements. They prefer to call this condition stromal edema nemoiosis.. Because this situation is very rare. We also agree with them that the name of stromatosis is Koyatar and this is the same classification. The diagnosis and the dangerous type as a meat product depending on the inner membrane of the uterus is also logical..

Symptoms and signs

In general, the symptoms of chronic pelvic swelling are low.. Since the course of the disease is variable, monitoring the patient for several months leads to an increase in accuracy in the diagnosis before surgery. Pelvic pain and tenderness that is not explained by infection or swelling must be the cause.

Endometriosis. When this diagnosis is tolerated, it is appropriate to keep this point in mind when evaluating abnormal bleeding, that excessive uterine bleeding is usually absent in external endometriosis and is present in the uterine lining. by finding a small swelling in the uterine joint of the sacral bone or in the same vicinity It means that the diagnosis of pneumiosis is usually not possible unless the samples are sent to a specialist.

In the section of the person's abdominal wall, usually non-neoplasmic. The tissue related to the inner membrane of the ovarian uterus develops, which itself contains a brown liquid.. Areas of burnt match" shape may be seen in the pelvic peritoneum. Dense adhesions result in the adhesion of permitted members. In some cases, the appendix is worm-like in accumulation .It is non-neoplastic and the tissue content related to the inner membrane of the uterus is attached..

Treatment

Endometriosis is a disease related to the reproductive period; Consequently, the treatment should be extremely careful. The following points should be considered: degree of symptoms, age, marital status, desire for Children, status of husband, fertility rate, presence of other pelvic diseases, possibility of distinguishing endometriosis, general physiological and psychological condition of the patient.. Since pregnancy has a very immediate and effective effect on endometriosis, young patients, even if they are suffering from the least degree Endometriosis must be clearly explained to them.. How is fertility?

If this is not acceptable, the patient and her husband should be carefully examined to find out the cause of the woman's infertility, and before opening the patient's abdomen, the cause of infertility should be treated immediately.

Treatment included

1 - Examination and insensitivity to pain - 2 - Sensation of egg drop by hormones   3 - It is a surgical operation. In the first stage, patients show very partial symptoms. It is absolutely necessary to examine the patient once every six months. Atminan and Sensations related to pain such as Darun and Idrisal have been effective in many cases.. Ovulation should be prevented with all skill by estrogen,

androgen or some other progesterones. Proponents of estrogen use believe that using high amounts of estrogen will prevent the production of follicle-stimulating hormones and the hormones that cause yellowing. And the ovarian function of the internal mucous gland becomes. The high amount of estrogen is the reason for the increase in the pelvic muscles and the softness of the fibrous adhesions and the increase in the absorption of the contents of the bag. It depends on the inner membrane of the uterus.

Karanaki proposed the method of large acetyl besterol and Cook reported good results.. Another program of treatment is by mouth and it is used three times a day after meals for five days in the following order: 1: mg, 2 mg, 3 mg, 5 mg, 10 mg, 15 mg and 25 milligram The last dose continues until the patient begins to bleed, at which time the dose increases to 50 mg per day. Recurrence of bleeding is a sign of the need to increase the amount of consumption per day to prevent bleeding. It is. This kind of great treatment continues for three months and then it is stopped. Some patients cannot tolerate the use of Acetyl bestrol due to nausea and vomiting, they also show some symptoms in the breasts and watery discharge from the vagina.

The main danger" Sudden stop" or excessive bleeding. Some of the patients have shown sensitivity to the effects of the aphrodisiac, and they have facial swelling or youthful pride, their voices are thick and deep, and a lot of hair starts to grow on their bodies because of the sedative effects. Liver disease is against the use of this method of treatment, and the appearance of jaundice shows that this treatment should be stopped. Methy ltestosterone or its equivalent, 5 to 10 mg, can be used daily for up to 60 days, and then until a menstrual period stops. However, this method is also a kind of waste of time.. After stopping the preventive treatment, the endometriosis areas become vascular and swollen again, and they again take the same form of periodic bleeding, as a result, the same specific symptoms occur again in the patient. does. with the existence of false pregnancy due to the use of an effective mixture of estrogen and progesterone (Enovid, which contains estrogen) is prescribed orally every day for two weeks, from.

The beginning of the fourth or fifth day of the menstrual period, the amount of daily consumption for two weeks after20 mg increments, then 30 mg daily for two weeks, and finally 40 mg Heat for the entire period that the treatment is necessary, which is usually between four and six months.. Such a special treatment of not bleeding from the uterus and also the effect of the mortal membrane for It causes endometriosis. According to his report, the sudden stop of bleeding was very low, but the severity Breast, weight gain, nausea and vomiting are some of its disturbing effects.. To prevent nausea and vomiting. it is better to take one pill with milk every night before going to bed.

At this moment, anti-convulsant and anti-vomiting medicine may also be required. Other effective progestins on the way Surgical treatment is recommended when, despite the measurement before surgery, the amount of treatment is not enough or the presence of accumulations in the pelvis is a sign of the possibility of neoplasm formation.. Partial intestinal obstruction has been seen almost less. In some cases, disturbing bleeding, dilatation and tearing and Careful examinations with anesthesia are necessary. Ovarian sacs attached to the inner lining of the uterus with a diameter of 5 to 6 cm are actually signs of the need for surgery because endometriosis can cause the destruction of the active ovarian tissues and possibly infertility. The principles of work conservation must be respected at all times. It is possible to separate the endometrioma from the ovary and from the valuable ovarian tissue with a single incision.

 The memory worked. In some cases, the tissue areas related to endometrioma can be cut or destroyed with the help of electric sparks. When the abdominal wall is torn, how does the uterus move? Hysteropexy is necessary. Cutting and taking out or a part of the tail before the bone Haji is performed when painful menstruation or painful intercourse occurs before surgery.

Removal of the organ in question with the preservation of the ovarian tissue has been considered as a surgical treatment in some patients. A complete hysterectomy and cutting both sides of the ovaries and fallopian tube is effective when it is not necessary to save the ovaries as an active organ, or due to the spread of the disease and stretching of the abdomen and intestines, such a removal is not required. In the past, external radiation was used for patients suffering from radiation sickness, but now, with the availability of female genital mutilation surgeons who can take cuts of any kind, other .There is no need for this action. The discomfort caused by radiation is Inability to get pregnant and the possibility of teuplasm being ignored in the adjacent organs or in the uterus..

 cysts and ovarian sacs

The natural size of the ovaries grows from childhood, the maturity of the sacs, the formation of the yellow body, the age of despair. And thinness is very variable. The naturalness of the ovary, such as the corpus callosum, the yellow corpuscle, and the sacs, is very important because they should not be mistaken for shaving the ovary or separating it.. Touching every time in years .The rule of having an accumulation in diameterconfirmed 5 cm, it is possible that this accumulation is a It is a neoplasm, in any case, it is good to continue the examination before its existence..

Non-neoplasmic cysts cellular cysts

With the cessation of egg shedding, the cell may be formed and grow, and these cells may be accompanied by abnormal bleeding or without it, and usually disappear between one and three months; But if its existence lasts more than three months and its diameter. The cut was 5 cm or more It is not necessary.

Yellow body bags

These sacs may accompany normal menstruation or pregnancy, and these sacs may cause the cessation of menstruation and irregular bleeding.. The treatment method is similar to the treatment of the bag It is a cell.

Yellow foot bags

Yellow pisces along with empty cysts and cancerous tumors caused by the skin of the mucous membrane of the diaphragm.

Polycystic ovarie

 Stein's ovaries- Luntal is one of the rare types, especially the ovaries. Most of them are accompanied by abnormal bleeding that should not be shaved or separated. Estrogen therapy to control bleeding may cause an increase in FSH and indirectly cause a decrease in ovarian volume.

Bags made of neoplasm

Simple bagsname "Simple bags" refers to bags with one hole or a smooth wall containing thin liquid or having a cube-shaped mucous membrane. These bags may be cell bags or watery cystadenoma. Despite the fact that most of them are small, some of them can be seen up to 10 to 25 cm in diameter. When their diameter is more than 5 cm meters, they should be shaved.

Aqueous cystadenoma

These bags may unnaturally cause the ovaries to expand or fill the abdominal cavity.. Their origin is the original mucous membrane of the ovaries and they may be single or multi-holed, with or without inflammation, and they are often seen in patients between the ages of 20 and 50. About 18% of them are bilateral. These are filled with a thin yellow matte liquid. Such types of swellings form a watery adenofibroma, which is harder than a bag. The path depends on the skin of the mucous membrane of a cubic shape and its types in its appearance in the form of irritation or dangerous types of this swelling. When it is seen coming near the bags, it is more likely to be in danger. When the parts of the ovary surface

Aqueous cystadeno carcinoma

 This situation is from two sides47% (Pemberton) and 71% (Taylor) cases have been seen, and it is the most well-known type of risk for the ovaries. Dangerous areas are in advanced risk areas and This dangerous condition may be present from the beginning of growth..

Pseudosinusoidal cystadenoma

Pseudomyosinous cystadenoma is slightly more than watery cystadenoma.. Single-hole types are less than multihole types. About 10% of these bags in their harmless type appear from two sides. Histological diagnosis shows the presence of long mucous membrane and columnar goblet cells, and their origin may be in neoplasmic elements. Its liquid is noticeably hard, thick and sticky, or it may be a thin liquid, in which case the growth cannot be cleaned from the types of serum. Areas of about 10% of this inflation. It has been done and it is likely that5% of it is also likely to become dangerous changes. The tearing of harmless types may be the cause of peritoneal culture and the development of pseudo myxoma depending on the peritoneum. The formation of a large amount of gelatinous elements in the stomach.

Pseudomyosinous cystadenocarcinoma

This stage includes about one third of the stages of general abtala and is probably bigger than Cistadu. It is aqueous carcinoma. Peritoneal-related pseudomyxoma compared to B-like disease. The risk of occurrence increases.

Ovarian miracle is a safe miracle

The harmless wonder is called dermoid cysts, and you can trace its existence from its large size because it has hair and fat that solidifies and hardens in the heat of the room.. There are many calcification areas and teeth may also be found in them. Histological studies confirmed the existence of adult organs of the skin and may include bony, cartilage, enteric, testicular, or thyroid elements, all of which in their adult state are cancerous tumors that are1 to 3% of cysts have been seen from the type of cells with a similar shape.. The accompanying benign tumor (one fifth of ovarian tumors due to neoplasm) occurs in 10% of cases.

There are two aspects of ovarian neoplasms in children, which have infinite different types.. As the tumor continues to develop, the natural tissue of the ovaries is destroyed. Since it can be identified very quickly from the oint of view of size, it is possible to cut it and remove it from the risk of destruction. He separated the body. Teratoma Teratoma usually means malignant teratoma, which is harder than cystic and includes. The centers of rapid tissue growth are the outer layer, the middle layer, and the inner layer of the three first embryonic layers.. The situation of two sides is such that even in children and young women, the ovaries or ovaries must be removed. brought out because the talent of this group of people is much more than old women..

Ovarian stroma

This name is applied when the thyroid tissue is teratoma, whether it is harmless or dangerous. overcome. The increase in the activity of the thyroid gland has been seen less. It goes away from teratoma.

Choriocarcinoma

Choriocarcinoma is a very rare ovarian tumor that is likely be taken. Two opinions have been expressed about the origin of teratomas: 1-Parthogenesis may happen. 2- One or more blastula cells may remain in the future gonad, and some of them are different depending on the type. The text will be in the form of multiple storage or hidden storage..

 Harmless hard swellings

Benign tumors of the ovaries, abnormal forms of neural tumors, tumors that are Blood or lymphatic vessels are removed, and the most famous of them are fibroma and Bernertiomer.. The last two swellings appear as white or small yellow streaks and small areas of bleeding in the cut areas. Under the microscope, you can check the characteristics of the skin cells of the mucous membrane of Bernarytomerez. Burner's tumors have been seen less often than fibroids and have been seen at least in postmenopausal women. Some bag and they are actually accompanied by pseudomyosinous cystadenoma.

Fibroma is usually small .It is possible to find many types of it. Abdominal distention and chest distention may also be seen along with this discomfort (Meggs discomfort symptoms community) gradual penetration and penetration of swelling. Maybe it is the main cause of discomfort and cutting it is the reason for preventing accumulation and fluid storage..Dangerous hard swellings, primary hard cancer tumors. This ovarian swelling is known as glandular carcinoma, tumorous carcinoma, medullary carcinoma, simple carcinoma, sacrificial carcinoma, perforated or pitted carcinoma, and reticular carcinoma. The location of mucous membrane skin cells, the number of related tissues, etc. from the point of view of characteristics .

It is histology. The origin of dangerous hard tumors is not known and half of them were bilateral. There are many areas of blood on the surface. Many of them are gray in color, combustible and perishable.

Mesonphroma

They believe that the mesonophroma is the mesonephric remains of the ovary.. The order of laying a pipe Hook-shaped cells with some tassel-like masses are its characteristic features..

Meat product

Egg meat product is very rare. Rapid growth and tissue corruption is one of its common factors. The prediction of the period of unhappiness is very weak. Dysgerminoma Dysgerminoma is one of the very rare tumors of the ovary, which is characterized by a semanoma related to the testis.. Most of them have been seen in children or young people. Basically, the growth is hard and has abundant density in the cut parts, the overall color tends to be gray. Although one-third of it is dangerous, if the ovary is not permeable, one-sided removal Ovaries are enough. Deep X-ray therapy may be a valuable aid to surgery in A case where the separation of the eggs is incomplete..

Active Amas

These estrogen producing tumors are yellow in surface section and their diameter is between1 cm to 15 cm or more, which may be bilateral bags, about 27% of the reported cases, or dangerous, about 25%, and in order to make a complete diagnosis, it needs a deep study. Before the start of the activity of the effective organs in menstruation and after the cessation of menstruation, the internal evidence of estrogen stimulation is a sign of its existence. Removal of one side of the ovary is appropriate in young women, however, in older women regardless of the appearance of the other ovary. It is necessary to cut both sides.

Theca cell carcinoma

Theca cell tumor is smaller and less dangerous than the squamous cell tumor.. Estrogen production produces similar clinical reactions. A firm amas with saccular regions, perhaps .It generally appears in the form of fibroma. Estrogen-producing tumors cause reproduction and increase the abnormal proliferation of the inner lining of the uterus. Ingraham and Novak believe that cancer related to the inner lining of the uterus is related to this. There will be amas.

Luteoma

Luteoma is a yellow cyst of the ovary, which may be a cell tumor. Be knowledgeable. Some of the luteoma that appears during pregnancy, considering the changes They come physiologically because they disappear by themselves.. Possible estrogenic and progestin effects They can be seen in the inner membrane of the uterus.

Arachnoblastoma

Arachnoblastoma is a male tumor that occurs in patients between It has been seen for 15 to 40 years. It cannot be said that all arachno blastomas produce androgens. It is strange that femininity(stopping bleeding, shrinking the size of breasts and hips) The occurrence of danger in the area It is 25%.

Amas of Rokliy

There are very few dress shirts and maybe it has a manly and regal force, or maybe it is the cause of Cushing's unhappiness in the society.. It is possible to increase the excretion of 17-ketosteroids, in Most of the times. While in arachnoblastoma, the discharge may be normal or slightly increased.. A dress is dangerous and two-way separation is necessary.

Gynandroblastoma

Gynandroblastoma is very rare and the reason for the occurrence of arachnoid blastoma along with the areas of cello-don-don or .It will be monotonous. As long as it is hormonally active, there is a possibility that the force of menstruation will prevail.

Cellular tumors in menstruation

These tumors are very rare and their origin may be from the lady cells of the testicles..

Metastatic ovarian cancer

Among the cancers related to the inner lining of the uterus,7% includes ovaries. It has been seen less that the cancer of the uterine body or uterine fibroids spread to the ovaries. Cancer related to the fallopian tube is often spread to the ovaries. Ovarian cancer may be the way of spreading the disease. be. A dangerous condition of the digestive system or breast cancer may spread to one or both ovaries. Grogenberg's tumors are caused by the cells of the vertebral ring (mucous). First wound is necessary.

Clinical diagnosis of non-active ovarian tumors

Benign and dangerous ovarian neoplasms have signs and symptoms from the beginning.. In general, it should be encountered when palpating the pelvis during a routine examination. (Initial examination for ovarian risk factors is the main reason for annual or six-monthly examinations for women aged 35 years and older). Abdomen is one of the duties for complete diagnosis. . Big ovarian sacs should be fromreach 15 cm or moreIt is possible to Qatar The abdomen and pregnancy should be cleaned well. Many times, the bags related to the pancreas are the cause. This is confusing. Small ovarian cysts (dermoid sacs) may be in front or behind the uterus. If they are not attached, they may rise from the pelvic cavity and move around when palpated. A bladder, gallbladder, or rectum is not full or swollen. Side pockets, liquid accumulation Water in the fallopian tube, complicated vein, accumulation of tubal pregnancy, pelvic floor, inverted uterus, intestinal or fat adhesions and specific fat or muscle may be the cause of creating problems or preventing the touch of the ovum..

Lack of complete rest due to fear or pelvic tenderness. It may e necessary to prevent the examination.

The complexity of the ovarian accumulations (side) compared to the wound is the main cause of pain. When the damage depends on the blood circulation leads to the death of the tissues of an area or blood spills into the accumulation, the person can experience pelvic pain. The occurrence of partial fever and an increase in the amount of cholestasis in the blood is usually followed by confusion and nausea.

Pain comes to the patient. Rupture of the ovarian sacs, whose contents may irritate the peritoneum, often causes abdominal pain. Fatty elements from harmless teratoma, when contact with the peritoneum is avoided for several days. If it is, it will have a very strong opposite effect. Bleeding may occur inside the ovarian tumor, which will be followed by frequent pain. Intra-abdominal bleeding and laceration of the veins are unlikely, but if the area becomes wider, it may cause shock. Intra-abdominal bleeding from areas affected by ulcers Although the inner membrane of the uterus is partial, it is painful.

The infection of the ovarian sacs is usually a sign of the continuation of the intestinal infection and the spread of the intestinal, tube or bladder infection.. If there is no complication, soreness, infection or bleeding from the pain .There is no news. It is possible for the patient to feel pressure and something falling from inside his body. Abdominal distention, large tumors, partial intestinal constipation lead to anorexia or constipation and weakness. Abdominal fluid should be studied to find malignant cells.. Menstrual period changes are less likely to happen unless there is a source of discharge. Ovarian endometrial sacs are an exception to this rule. Bleeding after menopause may happen with ovarian cancer, which is due to displacement of the uterus or possibility.

Changes in pelvic blood circulation. Displacement of ovarian cancer may be detectable in cold sores.. "The class neck"Inferior angle of choledochosac filled with cancer". Abdominal dissection is often the first Biopsy, may be enlarged or the contents of the cancer moved..It is an obvious sign of ovarian cancer.X-ray examination may show dermoid cysts, soft tissue accumulation in the pelvis. effective, and it may be the cause of kidney shadow to show pelvic pollen.. Urography or cystoscopy may be necessary. Proctoscopy, but Borum, the series related to the relationship between the intestine and the stomach are used when the patient is suspicious of ovarian cancer, and it is for this reason that it should be ruled out from the relationship with the intestine and the stomach in the first place. Keep it away.

Treatment

Excision is the general treatment of ovarian neoplasms.. If cysts in hair, fibroma, single-hole cysts with a smooth wall are definitely safe, the cyst may be excised and the natural tissue left in place. If the tumor has several holes and raised areas, it is necessary to separate it from the body. Cutting other ovaries (complete hysterectomy with surgical cutting of both sides of fallopian tube) is necessary when the dangerous end goal, the patient's age and her desire to get pregnant are carefully considered. Large and dangerous tumors may be removed from the body for temporary relief. If the disease has spread to the bladder or intestine, a biopsy may be performed first and then from X-ray treatment to hopefully ease the movement of the lumps to allow for more complete excision.

When peritoneal ovulation or abdominal dissection is seen, cytotoxin elements are injected into the peritoneum, as this method is more effective than radioactive gold, because Considering the transfer of related radioactive elements, it requires less cost and nursing care.. Thiotriethylen phosphoramide, as an alky l tinc component, is apparently the best opportunity for temporary relaxation. Chemotherapeutic agents may be injected intravenously or orally.

Chlorambucil should be used. These elements are very toxic and deadly and should be used with all caution and in the hands of qualified doctors due to hemopoietic degradation. X-ray therapy may be valuable, especially if targeted to an infected area, and may be used in conjunction with chemotherapy. Paracentesis is necessary in case of repeated abdominal resection. Prednisone According to the report, it is effective in reducing the formations related to peritoneal effusion.

If ovarian cancer can be removed before opening the ovarian surface, the chances of recovery are high. The poor diagnosis of ovarian cancer is mostly due to the multitude of symptoms. It is. Ovarian cancer is caused by weight loss, abdominal distension, anemia, blood and mood corruption, obstruction. Intestinal, the discharge is six times.

Prevention of ovarian cancer

Due to the insidious invasion of ovarian cancer tumors without showing specific symptoms, the patient thinks about treatment when the disease has advanced enough and the possibility of recovery is extremely weak.

To prevent the spread of this disease, Mrs. Brandaz, it is

better for the ovaries of women who reach the age of menstruation to be separated from the body, while the abdominal cavity remains for the activity of other active organs.. This opinion was criticized by Randall as the possibility of ovarian cancer was weak and he believed that Ovaries are very important for menopause and the years after that.. in separating the ovaries as a precautionary measure, which is the only way to prevent cancer There is a difference of opinion. Since 80% of dangerous ovarian disorders in Women above50 years old, it seems that separating the ovaries weak after menopause during hysterectomy is very popular and also the patient.

Estrogen support is not necessary in case of deficiency. Ovary removal before menopause from the point of view of natural estrogen deficiencies should be carefully considered, not only as a motivation to establish secondary sexual characteristics, but perhaps accompanied by less atherosclerotic and hypersclerotic changes. Considering the physiological effects of separating the ovaries in fertile women and men It is important.

Pregnancy tests Miscarriage

Miscarriage means getting pregnant before the embryo reaches the stage of development.. The name "inconclusive" is used by the public as the word "abortion" has a criminal aspect.. Since the appearance of miscarriage is true in patients who consult a doctor due to abnormal bleeding or pain, and also the possibility of disease of reproductive organs before pregnancy. Rood, accurate information about this matter is necessary for the treatment of gynecological diseases..

definition:

Classification of abortion should be based on the following points.

Natural abortion:

It is an abortion of a fetus that takes place naturally, i.e. Without the intervention of external factors. Induced abortion: It is an abortion that takes place on purpose. Sometimes, from the point of view of medical treatment, they abort the fetus to save the life of the mother. How can I do it without a doctor's prescription? It is considered a crime.

Abortion is threatening:

It is a stage where the patient has uterine bleeding or pain..

Abortion of the fetus is threatened:

It is a stage in which bleeding and pain have stopped.

Abortion of a defective fetus:

It occurs when a part of the pregnancy is outside the uterus.

Full abortion:

It is when all the products of pregnancy fall out of the uterus..

Abortion of an incompetent fetus:

It is performed when the sperm has grown or the fetus is dead and the uterus is.It is impossible to throw it out after eight weeks. Frequent abortion: It is the case that three pregnancies or more have been aborted naturally.

Scientific motivation

According to the statistics available in the United States10% of pregnancies lead to abortion. 50% of these people are due to sperm deficiency. In the abortion of the fetus in the first two months of pregnancy, 80% of the fetuses have defective growth. very time after studying

1000 natural abortions.

A sac-shaped obstruction has been seen in most of them.. Other causes of natural abortion include swelling malnourishment, syphilis, neck cultivation, laceration and cut or compression of the umbilical cord.. The possible role of hormonal imbalance, internal disorders, and the inner lining of the uterus that has not grown properly may be an important symptom in some pregnancies. A lot of miscarriages in a way .It happens that you can't find out how it happens with normal tests.. Abortion of the fetus may be caused by placing foreign objects such as metal or wooden objects in the uterine cavity. To speed up childbirth, using drugs orally or subcutaneously will not have an effect on quick natural childbirth. In the same way, if the delivery is natural, exercise or heavy sports will cause miscarriage. Radiation on the growing sperm or embryo in the first stages of growth, if it is concentrated enough, it will cause the growth to stop and will soon lead to the abortion of the embryo. Using elements to treat leukemia and others .Dangerous drugs may lead to abortion.. Surgery on the uterus in progress Pregnancy has caused an increase in the stimulation of muscle swelling and may cause abortion of the fetus. to any Now, neck biopsy and heating of the uterus rarely cause pregnancy discomfort..

Pathology

Hemorrhage and infection are major stages of pathology. The amount of shed blood is very different and sometimes the cause of death is due to anemia. Bleeding is possible from the culture center or from .Let the mortal membrane be clear. It is possible to see blood loss and mortal membrane corruption, gradual corruption of the fetus, menstrual irregularity, genital malformation, placental atrophy, sac-like changes in the shape of the trophoblast. When the separation of trophoblast is completed, the bleeding stops. and the mortal membrane falls out. How much trophoblast remains in the form of adhesions?

The possibility of bleeding is very high. Corruption may be related to the product of conception and mortal membrane; because by pulling the lymphatics, it can lead to the swelling of the free tissue between the two layers and sometimes swelling of the bee tissues. It is possible to attack the blood circulation with the development of pus-producing thrombophlebitis in the pelvis. As the progress of the occurrence of the boil, especially in the six and finally in all the body parts, it should be pulled.. If the infection spreads to the fallopian tube, the possibility of severe fallopian tube and peritoneal abscess is extremely high.

The death that often follows the abortion of the fetus is usually due to severe peritonitis, or the presence of deadly bacteria in the blood, or abscesses moved in the It is other parts of the body. When a missed miscarriage occurs at fourteen weeks of pregnancy, the possibility of spreading hypofibryogenmia is very high. If there is severe bleeding or shock, or if there is any infection. If it is too much, it will lead to kidney nephrosis ..diagnosis For menstrual irregularities and recurrent uterine bleeding during the first weeks of pregnancy, there may or may not be evidence of amenorrhea in a patient who is likely to miscarry.. In a disease that can become pregnant, the observation of irregularities in uterine bleeding makes a person think of the possibility of abortion. When excessive uterine bleeding occurs without a specific reason, the best reason and explanation.

If some blood is seen, the diagnosis will be infinitely simpler and almost certain.. In general, the pain accompanying the abortion of the fetus is in the form of muscle contraction and twisting. It is possible in pelvic examination If the pregnancy has progressed sufficiently, the softening and enlargement of the uterus should be observed.. It is soft and abundant. The expulsion of any tissue from the uterus should be carefully reviewed. As soon as a certain amount of the mortal membrane or the falling membrane of the uterus is separated, the abortion of the fetus is inevitable. It is. The appearance of a healthy placental sac or a complete uterine prolapse is the best evidence of complete fetal abortion.

It is. As the absence of trophoblast growth appears earlier than usual, pregnancy tests may not be positive. If there is sufficient chronic gonadotropin production to confirm the test. this positive state may remain for one or two weeks even though sperm growth has stopped.. When the pre-pregnancy test is positive before the size of the uterus is equal to the week of pregnancy. On the 16th day of pregnancy, the possibility of miscarriage is temporarily stopped..

To arrange

When a miscarriage is diagnosed, the patient should be instructed to limit physical movements and prescribe sedative and sedative drugs.. Examinations are necessary to determine the cause of the symptoms in the patient who may have other conditions such as active uterine bleeding, bleeding from neoplasia, illegitimate pregnancy or no bleeding in the peritoneal cavity. Since the majority of early-stage abortions are not caused by hormones, hormone therapy is recommended for less morbidity.

The patient should avoid showering and sexual intercourse as much as possible to avoid the "possibility" of tissue shedding. Re-examinations are necessary to confirm the progress of pregnancy. If the bleeding is recurring and the uterus is about to grow, prescribing progesterone through the muscle or artificially through the mouth may be important. In the case of no uterine expansion, it is possible to detect the abortion of the forgotten fetus. Of course, this is in the case that the diagnosis of pregnancy has already been made..Forgotten abortion can only be detected if the patient is repeatedly examined.. Many times, the soft swelling of the uterine muscle is the reason for the proportional expansion of the uterus, and sometimes the fat and the location of the uterus may interfere in the measurement of the size of the uterus; As a result, in such a case, the diagnosis of forgotten abortion is not free of problems. In this kind of abortion, it is better to get help from the force of nature.

As long as the uterine cavity is not invaded, there is no risk of infection. The risk of hypofibrinogenemia that develops along with an abortion of an old fetus. He finds that it should be taken seriously, even though there are very few such cases.. A miscarriage is unavoidable when the uterine body has fully expanded, even though none of the pregnancy organs and the uterine membrane have fallen out. Determining the abortion of an unviable fetus. Avoidance based on the amount of blood loss alone cannot be error free.. permission Medicines to speed up childbirth, such as Syntosion, by intramuscular injection, lead to the inevitable result.. When the pregnancy is twelve weeks or less, shaving after emptying and emptying the uterus with the help of surgical forceps may be effective in preventing bleeding.

If the pregnancy period exceeds twelve weeks, it is better to pass through the uterus without the use of labor facilities due to the size and volume of the growing sperm and embryo. Surgery will be arranged. Most of the patients suffering from premature or incomplete abortion have vaginal bleeding. The symptoms may stop and reappear a few days later. In order to prevent more blood loss and disability,

Anti-inflammatory content against tetanus and bacteremia should be prescribed.. When an infectious miscarriage occurs, the patient usually suffers from chills and severe fever. While touching, it is possible to identify the areas of stiffness with specific tenderness. A little tenderness may be seen without uterine infection in other types of abortion. It is possible that there are elements to accelerate childbirth.

but the attack on the uterus is prevented so that the natural barriers to prevent infection are given a chance.. With the help of X-ray film, the patient should be examined for evidence of an infectious body blocking the blood flow in the vein. Cultures must be obtained from the uterus and blood. Infectious shock needs muscle and blood vessel constrictors for shock relief due to the effects of gram-negative bacillus endotoxin. As long as the infection did not show any effect on the antibacterial treatment for a certain period of time, in some patients, the blood vessels were closed.The big black vein or the vena cava and the ovarian veins are the cause of saving them from the danger of death.. When miscarriage happens repeatedly, the uterus should be carefully examined for the possibility of defective or distorted birth, and this may require hysterography. In most cases of hysterograms .It also causes rough myositis of the mucosa.. Inadequacy and incompetence of the inner cervix is revealed by quick and almost painless abortion after fourteen weeks of pregnancy, and sometimes in non-pregnant women, it can be detected with the help of touching the uterine cavity or by inserting the uterus. The expansion of the number10. It is possible to recognize the same thing without resistance. Hysterography is a more reliable method.

It has been recommended to repair the cervix with the help of a triangular incision and suturing its upper part in non-pregnant women. Shirodker and also Barter and his colleagues suggested the placement of "a bag whose head is closed by pulling a thread" and cannot be absorbed submucosally around the cervix in order to protect the cervix from dilatation of the pregnancy unit. Others suggest that a deep cervical burn resulting from an injured burn or placing a Hodge-type uterine band should be used to hold the cervix from the back. The surgeon prefers to repair a crooked or defective uterus. All this method in selected patients The result is satisfactory.

Determining the timing of hormonal or vitamin therapy in the treatment of miscarriage is quite difficult.. When he could not determine the cause, prescribing mineral elements, vitamins, thyroid extract and Progesterone has many supporters before and after pregnancy.. In recent years Hydroxyprogesterone caproite in oil, nortin pills, pills Nortinodrel has been prescribed during pregnancy and miscarriages have been reported..It is known to be used by word of mouth. Its lack of androgenic effects for long-term use Longer duration is more desirable, because symptoms of hemorrhaging of growing sperm have been reported with high use of hydroxyprogesterone caproite. Since there is no test to determine whether there is enough progesterone in the patient in question or not, and most doctors are unaware of it, additional progesterone should only be given in relation to a previous pregnancy and through experience and with consideration of blood. Pregnancy should be considered. The method of adequate and long-term rest and relaxation in order to prevent early abortion or to avoid heavy work seems to still have a lot of value in the important issue of abortion. The method of suggestions and continuous indoctrination of psychiatrists is also an important help for pregnant women and it is possible to protect their fetuses.. Adequate attention to infections and hard kidney cysts may increase the patient's ability to bear pregnancy. Other cases, such as the spread of arteriosclerotic ulcers and pelvic tuberculosis in patients suffering from Miscarriages show less symptoms. Unexpected pregnancy .

An ectopic pregnancy means an illegitimate pregnancy, usually outside the uterus, and often it is a tubal pregnancy.. other place The places where the egg may be pulled are:: (1) uterine horns (2) ovaries (3) broad ligaments (4) abdomen (5) cervix. The third and fourth numbers are considered as secondary centers.. Number five according to his report Less has happened. It will be 6/107. The occurrence of these cases was higher in the black race of Pustan, and more pelvic infections were extracted in the black race than in the white race. have been. Considering the increase in the birth rate in recent years, it is obvious that there are measures to Death has also been prevented.

Pathology

The main change from the point of view of pathology is bleeding. The endosalpinx has grown and invades the wall of the tube and its blood vessels.. Some of the stromal cells related to the endosalpinx undergo changes depending on the prolapsed membrane, but the Nitabukh cell, which is formed naturally in the inner lining of the uterus, is not visible. The blood flow in the tissue of the body first started through the subcutaneous mucosa and It separates some active tropholast from the blood.

With the continuation of bleeding, the blood causes the capsules to be inflated and their separation from the fusion or the external placenta. It becomes a fetus. That is, when the capsules containing tubular mucous membrane, fibrin and some tears of the falling membrane cells break, the blood spreads inside and is drawn into the tubular channel. If the bleeding does not take place from the fallopian tube of the peritoneal cavity or the wide junction, the term "unseen tubal pregnancy" is more common. From Where the tube expands rapidly and tries to expel its contents, it hurts.

Parzuri touches the patient. This intense pain along with twisting may also be caused by uterine contractions at this stage. After intraductal tear, blood drips from the rooted end of the tube into the peritoneal cavity. Bleeding from the center of the culture is not drawn to the cavity connected to the inner membrane of the uterus, except for intramural pregnancies. What a complete separation Crack or hair growth depending on the fusion or external placenta of the fetus, clots of the product. Pregnancy and the blood related to it, in the form of abortion of the fetus, fall into the abdominal cavity. However, tubal abortion is rarely seen as complete.. Gradual corruption of trophoblast may be the cause of interference and penetration of the fluid membrane or aqueous humor along with bleeding and from there it goes directly into the cavity. With sufficient corruption of the pipe wall It may be the cause of venous pressure and cause full vision..

The amount and time of bleeding in the culture center is different. When the pregnancy is in the inner part of the wall of the fallopian tube, the muscular lining of the uterus that surrounds it allows the growth of the point to progress for three months or more until the gradual destruction of the endometrium with sudden bleeding begins. The narrow part or neck of the fallopian tube is not easily dilatable and gradual corruption through the tube usually starts in 6 weeks or less with noticeable bleeding.

The tube-shaped part of the ampoule is expandable and pregnancy is likely to be longer than the narrow part; However, it sometimes happens that the rupture of one of the large arteries causes rapid bleeding. Since the amount and extent of bleeding in the center of the tumor varies, the pain resulting from tubular dilatation or peritoneal stimulation of blood outside the normal duct also varies. The more blood spills into the abdominal cavity, the pain may go to the upper part of the abdomen or stimulate the diaphragm. It is the reason why the pain spreads to the shoulders.

The trophoblast hormone product is cut off when it is separated from the active blood source.. If estrogen and progesterone are not produced enough, the inner membrane of the uterus sheds. Usually, the deficiency of hormone production is gradual and intermittent so that the bleeding from the inner membrane of the uterus is also intermittent and low. Sometimes, due to sudden defects in the secretion of the falling membrane of the uterus, it may come out in the form of an incomplete or complete miscarriage. After the uterine bleeding lasted for several days, I gave birth.

The inner membrane of the uterus, which undergoes the changes of the falling membrane of the uterus, usually sheds and studies. The rest of the uterus does not show any traces of pregnancy. Breast changes and breast tenderness depend on the sufficient production of secretory elements and are possible in the same order. It is due to the bleeding inside the sausage-like duct that changes the shape of the heart.. Fetus, placental sac. The embryo and the embryo may continue to grow and form a mass that may be intratubal or extratubal.. Storage of blood clot and liquid blood is possible through the intestine. Adhesion of the larynx and the members of the lateral reproductive organs becomes a pseudocyst.. With the hardening of this Watery swelling of the limb soon appears as blood reabsorption begins. As long as this period lasts, the blood supply will become infected.. If the separation of trophoblast is cut off from the active blood source, tissue corruption has started and it can be cured by absorbing the products of pregnancy.

It is possible that the aborted sperm was poured into the stomach.. Then the trophoblast finds a new adhesion site to attach to the adjacent organs. in such Abdominal pregnancy has been established and may continue to grow under certain conditions.. Ovarian pregnancy occurs when the culture is done in a ruptured bag or on the level of the ovary. Of course, this situation rarely happens. As mentioned in the third chapter, the first uterine horns may be the defective center for pair formation and the reason

Symptoms and diagnosis

Symptoms depend on various factors, and these factors include the center, type, and condition of the unit. External pregnancy and final initial pain and general condition of the patient. In general, you should be a doctor Diagnose the accumulation of blood in the peritoneal cavity and look for abdominal accumulation..It is possible for the patient to refer to the doctor due to the observation that the bleeding has stopped.. The patient may be suffering from confusion, breast discomfort and periods without burning, or maybe none of these discomforts will appear in him. In case of this discomfort Yes, the softness of the neck and the discoloration or discolouration of the vagina is accompanied by pregnancy.. Partial expansion Rahmi can be discovered if the treating doctor has seen the patient before.. Pain due to the movement of the cervix should make a person think of an ectopic pregnancy. The doctor should touch the adjacent organs very slowly and carefully, and while touching, the accumulation should be small and soft, and at the same time, he should try to tear the yellow body of pregnancy or The uterine tube does not become pregnant.

If a pregnancy test (Qorbaghe for Friedman-Lapham) is necessary Therefore, the obtained result should be carefully evaluated, considering that a negative answer is not a sign of ectopic pregnancy or the first uterine pregnancy, and a positive answer of the test indicates the presence of a crack or the special irritation of the hair in the vagina. Circulation is mother's blood. In doubtful cases that are free of any abdominal symptoms, the patient should be examined periodically for a period of one to two weeks, so that a certain diagnosis can be confirmed. At such a stage, a person may suspect illness. If the lower abdominal pain continues, the doctor should try to remove the fluid. It should be taken from the right cut of the uterus by piercing the vaginal wall.

A negative answer indicating the absence of tubal pregnancy is not healthy.. Examination of one A choledoscopy specialist is very effective in such cases.. If the tests cause The revelation of the soft tubular accumulation and the uterus cannot expand as it should, expands as it should. The pregnant woman expands and expands. A choledotomy or a cut of the abdominal wall is necessary.. It is obvious that the blood type and Rh-Hr status of each patient should be taken as precautionary measures. be taken into account. 2- In cases of tubal abortion or rupture without acute symptoms of the disease, as Adi is not readable. In addition, the following cases may not be exempted from this rule.

Symptoms of pregnancy, weight loss, weight loss as a symptom of pelvic pain, diagnosis of vaginal bleeding symptoms and symptoms of general weakness, headache or confusion .It may be touchable and it may not be. As soon as the uterus is touched, the patient feels pain and a positive fluid is drawn out from the rectal incision of the uterus with a puncture.

The anterior vaginal wall is diagnosed. In patients suspected of miscarriage, cervical dilatation and uterine incision cause the contents of the uterus to be revealed, and if the diagnosis is correct, it leads to the patient's recovery. Romney and his colleagues proved that the studies related to the endometrium in ectopic pregnancy are not reliable because the endometrium is from a stage of initial development to the stage related to the falling or secretion of the uterine membrane. It is constantly changing and these changes are different in different people and in different cases of a single person.: The presence of a crack or the growth of furun hair or external mesima. Fetus in shaving is a sign that the patient had an intrauterine pregnancy. But this

Peritoneal cavity

Uterine bleeding, uterine bleeding, and slight uterine enlargement, unless the patient is suffering from swelling or pregnancy; A lateral accumulation or cold sore may be palpable, depending on the patient.. Extraction of liquid from the rectal incision of the uterus by piercing the vaginal wall is positive if the patient is suspicious of the existence of blood invasion in the peritoneal cavity; In such cases, the drawn blood should be monitored for at least six minutes.

If this blood is from the peritoneal cavity that does not want to clot, but if If it is from a blood vessel, it closes in the same minimum time, except in cases of blood disorder.. The shedding of small amounts of old blood is interpreted as positive. 4- The fourth type, which is called pelvic blood collection or ruptured ectopic pregnancy, can be identified, provided that a person searches for records that correspond to a recent tubal rupture or fetal abortion.

This situation may have been created several weeks before the settlement. due to recurrent lower abdominal pain, recurrent uterine bleeding, pain to move the uterus, limitation of the amount of uterine oscillation, accumulation of pelvic soft tissue and maybe erythrocyte sedimentation rate, fever, etc., the following points should be carefully considered:

Separating the ovaries of the fallopian tubes(PID), fallopian tube abscess, endometriosis, endometrial abscess, abortion of defective fetus in "fixed" uterus, ovarian sac and dangerous cases. Some patients have one or more of these symptoms in addition to accumulation. They are pelvic blood. If the patient is suspected of having a boil, choledotomy is effective and It helps in correct diagnosis.

Treatment

Unintended pregnancy should be treated with surgery without wasting time.. Veins that caused bleeding.A spinal cord is often performed in the case of patients who have little or no blood in the peritoneal cavity, considering the risk.. In the case of suspected ectopic pregnancy, sufficient blood should always be available to the doctor and this blood should not be used to cure anemia.

It is. In the case of abdominal shock, while the patient is using the oxygen mask, it should be opened and through the arteries, enough blood can be delivered to the patient's body (Serini vein) until the blood pressure and the contraction of the heart and arteries are higher than 90 mm. The mercury reaches and the lead depends on the pulse and becomes palpable to the higher life. He continued the treatment. In cases of severe tearing accompanied by accumulations resulting from Bleeding during surgery should be limited to the organs adjacent to the uterus.. The ovaries of one side should be preserved as much as possible. The opposite tube and ovary should be carefully inspected to ensure whether there is a neoplasm pregnancy, or a compensable tubal condition or not, the general condition of the patient should be good, and the breakdown of adhesions in the internal organs should be included and selected. Therefore, returning the dilation of the fallopian tubes will not harm the possibility of future pregnancy. If the patient has lost the opposite fallopian tube or has been damaged in a part that cannot be repaired, it is possible to separate the pregnancy product from the fallopian tube in such a way as to cause its release to some extent. The recurrence of ectopic pregnancy is considered to be between 3% and 5% of all patients under the test. This rate is found in the patient who is under the tuberoblast.

Common types of foreign pregnancies

A doctor who considers the possibility of an ectopic pregnancy in his patient should not do the following: Intramural pregnancy(Muscular gap). Bleeding is due to extreme pain. In some cases, the fallopian tube can be surgically separated or that part of the uterus.It is attacked by a disease. In other cases, the uterus should also become a victim of this disease.

Ovarian pregnancy

Although it is rarely seen, the symptoms of ovarian pregnancy are similar to tubal pregnancy. And there is a high probability of rupture of the yellow body sac, complication and inflammation of the inner uterine membrane..

Abdominal pregnancy

There are very few cases that prove the early stages of this type of pregnancy.. In the secondary stages, the problem of miscarriage or tearing occurs. Inversion or other abnormal forms of the fetus should be the reason for the stimulation.

It may be longer than normal pregnancy. Different parts of the fetus can be touched directly under the abdominal wall or the back part of the vagina. If the body of the uterus is tilted up and forward due to the accumulation of pregnancy, the posterior part of the uterus is close to the connection and its exact location. A rapid pregnancy test may reveal the absence of the uterus around the fetus.. to your help Arteriography may visualize the fetal pair.. In some cases, Simpson's tube is used to measure the depth of the uterus, but if there is a possibility of pregnancy, this tube should not be used. In general, patients with abdominal pregnancy should be immediately surgery will be performed, because if the growth of the sperm is in the ..It is a diagnosis and a statement that according to the opinion of the doctors, a certain time should be set aside to be able to provide and inspect the blood for consumption.. The blood needed by the patient should be available in sufficient quantity be. Lithopendion is very rarely seen in the United States.

Trophoblastic diseases

A shaped bagAccumulation

A small part of all the hair growths or the external placenta of the fetus that are formed during a pregnancy may undergo gradual spontaneous degeneration to turn into sac organs.. A slight change in the sac often occurs spontaneously in early miscarriage. Almost strange It is possible that there is a significant amount of sac change in the fetus of one pregnancy.. when Most of the growths of the hairs of the external cervix of the fetus turn into sac organs. The general situation of this accumulation is a bunch of grapes. When such a stage is reached, a grown sperm or an embryo is rarely found, of course, even if the sac changes to the required level, there is not enough nutrition for the growth of the sperm.

Accumulations of bag shaped approximately between1 in 500 to 1 in 2500 pregnancies are estimated. Under the microscope, the hair growths are considered very large, without fluff, and the trophoblast has more growth compared to normal pregnancy. According to Hertik's report, 5.73% of bag accumulations are in a safe stage; That is, it did not attack the vaginal wall unnaturally and Or they don't spread to other body parts.

Symptoms, evidence, diagnosis

A pregnancy that is doomed to accumulation is similar to a normal pregnancy in the invasion phase.. Often the first discomfort is a runny nose and sometimes it is accompanied by bleeding. In the examination, in almost the majority of such cases, the scale of uterine dilation is considered to be many times higher than that of a normal pregnancy. When the volume of the uterus is equal to the size of the pregnancy from 18 weeks to 22 weeks, the X-ray test and listening to the internal sounds of the body do not show any trace of the existence of the fetus. Accumulations that take this amount of albuminous urine, abnormal expansion and watery swelling are possible. increase. Often, the presence of accumulation is considered as a sign of the presence of an aqueous bag. If the womb is sufficient.

if it is expanded and there is no trace of the fetus, the doctor may insert the surgical forceps into the uterine cavity and begin to diagnose by removing a small amount of the sac.. An abnormal gonadotropin-trophoblast product, when carefully examined, usually looks more like a normal pregnancy; However, as a gonadotropin product, it is possible to reach the highest level, more than 200,000 units of mice from six to ten weeks, until several Do not repeat for a week, the person will pay less attention to this scale..

Arrange

Once the diagnosis of cystic fibrosis is complete, tissue evacuation is required for treatment. It is an accumulation of the uterus. The wall of the uterus may be briefly invaded, as a result, it needs a lot of attention. Fingers and sponge tongs can also be used for cutting tools. Work will come. in the near10% accumulations can be found by touching the adjacent organs that the ovaries are larger than normal and this characteristic is due to the lutein sacs that form the gonadotropin stimulation. In the absence of large bags, study histology. It shows a lot of yellowness.

After the trophoblastic tissue was separated, these changes .If it has reached the first stage, it is better to remove the accumulation as an abdominal hysterectomy, which allows for more visualization and inspection of the uterus and faster removal of the abdominal pregnancy tissue.. It is better for patients who have given birth to multiple births and suffer from accumulation and are prone to the growth of cancerous tumors of the mucous membrane of the outer placenta of the fetus. The first opportunity is to undergo a full abdominal hysterectomy..

As long as the uterus is not separated, it is necessary that the subsequent examinations be done regularly at least once a year to determine the possibility of cancerous tumor of the mucous membrane of the outer placenta of the fetus due to accumulation. During this period, the patient should be careful of pregnancy. The gonadotropin test (pregnancy test) should be done once every two weeks until the answer is negative, and from that moment the patient will be tested once every two months for one year.

A negative test showed a positive answer again, and if there is no possibility of a new pregnancy, the probability The spread of cancerous tumors of the mucous membrane of the external placenta of the fetus is very high.. If in Returning the uterus to its normal state, if there is a defect or if there is abnormal bleeding following the removal of the accumulation, it is necessary to repeat the excision.. As he could not prevent the bleeding Hysterectomy is usually the best solution. Carcinoid tumors of the mucous membrane of the external placenta of the fetus .This extremely dangerous cancer of trophoblastic cells is very rare.. The probability of its occurrence is 1 in 25,000 pregnancies. From cancerous tumors of the mucous membrane of the cervix. The outside of the fetus that was discovered is about50% for bag-shaped stacking, 25% for Miscarriage and25% were looking for periodic pregnancy.

The diagnosis of this disease depends on finding. it is the tissue of the patient that must be carefully examined from the histological point of view.. from the point of view. The clinical diagnosis of this disease is possible at first by the sound of the displaced wound in the bone, bone, The brain, liver, vagina, or organs related to the stomach and intestines appear.. These wounds may cause pain or bleeding. An enlarged uterus that is not twisted and the bleeding stops after a natural pregnancy abortion should be suspicious of this disease.

As mentioned above, in patients suffering from cystic fibrosis, it is recommended to shave the uterus. With the spread of cancerous tumors of the outer placental mucous membrane of the fetus, which may happen weeks or even years after pregnancy, none of the cancerous tissues are visible when scraping. In fact, when the trophoblastic cells are scraped to the hand A pathologist is hesitant to determine the exact position of the uterus.. Cystictioma is completely harmless,

 it is self-limiting and may be accompanied by vaginal bleeding and uterine incompetence. Its distinctive feature is the presence of trophoblastic tissue in the embryonic center when it is dissected. Only female genital pathologists are allowed. When diagnosing this situation, do not mistake it for a dangerous situation.. Cleaning the skin membrane Mucous membrane of the external placenta of the fetus and cancerous tumors of the mucous membrane of the external placenta of the difficult fetus It is. This condition is a local invasion of bag-shaped accumulation along with displaced wounds.

It will happen, especially in six. It is in such a situation that the uterus becomes much larger than the cancerous tumor of the mucous membrane of the external placenta of the fetus. During a careful examination and testing, it is possible to find the existence of an aspiration hair growth that has sunk deep into the layers of the muscular skin of the uterus. After separating the pelvic wounds by hysterectomy, sometimes the wounds Six also disappear. Most of the time, cancerous tumors of the mucous membrane of the external placenta of the fetus cause the blood serum to have a high standard of gonadotropins. Undoubtedly, when there is a cancerous tumor of the external mucous membrane of the fetus, the determination of the quality of gonadotropins should be done.

The treatment of cancerous tumors of the external mucous membrane of the fetus is a complete hysterectomy and the removal of the bilateral fallopian tubes, which should be followed by X-ray treatment in the pelvis and each Use another part that has spread disease.. Nitrogen mustard as a treatment .Accommodation is recommended for the transfer of illness. Hertz and his colleagues controlled some displaced wounds by using a high amount of methotrexate, resulting in temporary relief in most patients. They have reported it.

Predicting the period of unhappiness

Sac accumulations are less likely to lead to death, and death is often due to uterine bleeding.. Death is also possible due to an aggressive accumulation in which bleeding may be the only. It should be through the vagina, but also into the peritoneal cavity after being pushed out of the uterine wall.. Carcinoma of the foreskin of the mucous membrane of the external placenta of the fetus, usually through hemorrhage and corruption in The active tissues of the body cause the death of the patient.

Disorders of active members

Natural prevention of uterine discharge(especially the secretion of the inner lining of the uterus) in the first chapter in detail .It has come. Some known changes in appetite and other activities that cause active disorders that .If it is not mentioned in other parts of this collection, it will be discussed in this chapter..

Stop bleeding

Stopping bleeding can be classified as follows.: (1) the primary one in which the rule or tamath has not been revealed (2) in which after the establishment of the activity The rules of the rule ortamath are revealed.

Hereditary abnormalities

The discussion of lack of uterus or ovaries, vaginal obstruction, different forms of genitals is discussed in the third chapter.. The mucosal stages of stopping bleeding are as follows :Mucous matters.

Hypopituitarism

Chromophobic adenoma related to mucosa may compress the basophilic elements of the gland.. If this condition occurs during childhood, it will lead to short stature, and if it occurs in adults, it will stop bleeding, thin the genitals, reduce the amount of transformation, and "ShockSymonds disease may follow acute infection or Strength is one of its consequences. midwifery" Be it. Cancer tumors of the mucous membrane of the skin or cysts may cause the destruction of the pituitary gland. Anorexia nervosa can appear in severe mucosal lesions and have a positive effect on the face treatment.

It is different from Symonds disease.

Basophil pituitary tumor(Cushing's syndrome)

Basophilic pituitary tumor along with fat body, face and neck interferes with ovarian function by creating additional activity of adrenal gland.. The amount of OH17 - costosteroids increases He finds. This swelling is very rare, because most patients with Cushing's syndrome do not have swelling. They are mucous membranes.

Acidophilic mucosal abscesses

These tumors may cause abnormal growth, and this is if it is already closed. Apophyses will develop, or it may cause acromegaly in adults Bleeding, weight gain, excessive sweating, lethargy and impotence, hairiness or excessive hair growth, excessive pigmentation in the skin tissues, and the presence of sugar in the urine are some of the symptoms. It is characteristic.

Adiposogenital dystrophy(Fröhlich syndrome)

This disease is an irregularity in the active members of the mucosal area of the encephalon, fat in It gathers around the waist, breasts, thighs, arms and buttocks.. Stop bleeding or defects There is a lot of bloodshed; However, increased blood loss or intramuscular bleeding is also possible. It has to be updated.

lack of FSH

lack ofFSH along with the abnormal defects of the activity of the gland and growth glands of the reproductive organs and the slowness of sexual growth may appear without a specific reason. In Chiari-Fromel syndrome, bleeding, excessive and spontaneous secretion of milk, FSH deficiency, emaciation and dryness of the uterus, ovaries and vagina after a natural pregnancy may be related to nutritional deficiencies or disorders.

Thyroid cases- Hyperadrenalism is the cause of menstruation due to androgenic effects. will be. Adrenal hyperplasia can be treated with cortisone, hydrocortisone, prednisone, Prednisolone or dexamethasone should be adjusted. If the cause is neoplasia, corticoids are used Androgen yield correction and additional product have no role. When the degrees are weak and low Abnormal extra secretory activity of the gonads is suspected, a therapeutic trial of cortisone or its homodiffer mixture in a very small amount may result in normal ovarian function. In addition, the egg will fall. When hypoadrenalism occurs, bleeding stasis is one of its characteristic symptoms..

Ovarian stages

Severe destruction of ovarian tissue by infection, tumors, radiation or surgical intervention due to some reason. Qassan produces estrogen, which causes bleeding to stop.. Stein-Lonthal syndrome is less common. Ovaries full of sacs on both sides with stasis of bleeding; with a yield without egg shedding and sometimes woolly with a dubious origin and A dressing is usually prescribed for the treatment of hyperadrenalism, but in the society of unpleasant symptoms. Rare seeds are less productive. Hormonal tissue studies revealed the reason for one Biosynth Zeiss along with increasing the amount of Androstanedione, a testosterone precursor, which Pashmalui account and increase17 Ketosteroids are placed in patients.

The involuntary failure of immature ovaries can be diagnosed as follows (1) the absence of ovarian diseases (2) the reaction of the endometrium to stimulation (3) normal or excessive levels of FSH. This condition can become serious in women in their early years From the point of menstrual symptoms Immature ovaries are similar to adult ovaries..

Physiological matters- Physiological cases of bleeding stasis include the following causes:　　　(4 search and search before (3) The search and the khaiz period of youth and puberty(2 Menstruation(1 pregnancy (7) Changes in weather and　　(6) Temporary emotional disorders(5) milk secretion menstruation eight.

Medical cases

Stop bleeding may be the result of previous treatment.. There is no doubt in the surgical cut. The use of a small amount of X-ray radiation in the ovaries may temporarily stop the bleeding, while the use of a higher amount is the same as used in the treatment of cancer. There is a permanent stop of bleeding and loss of ovaries.. Using a sufficient amount of radium in the membrane.

The inside of the uterus causes complete weight loss. Continued use of estrogen can be high It causes bleeding for three months or more.. It is possible to mix estrogen and progesterone This is the reason for prolonged bleeding. Diseases that lead to the patient's disability, lymphoma and severe malnutrition are possible causes. They are stasis bleeding. Abnormal uterine bleeding The stages of abnormal uterine bleeding are as allows.: Excessive bleeding- Abnormal menstrual bleeding (eruption) Bleeding defects - Low bleeding during menstruation, abnormal menstrual cycle - Excessive menstruation Bleeding between two periods- Bleeding except during menstruation (bleeding during enstruation). The egg is also of this type, but this condition is only for one or two days. It turns out that it is also due to estrogen deficiency.

the cause- The following are the causes of abnormal uterine bleeding:

Uterine bleeding due to lack of proper activity

Irregular, excessive, low or prolonged uterine bleeding without neoplasia, infection, pregnancy, injury as a result of a wound, blood disorder or secretion order is a cause that is called true inactivity.. For diagnosis, past or physical examinations should not indicate the mentioned discomforts. . Biopsy depending on the inner membrane or expansion and shaving and laboratory studies including It is necessary.

When the diagnosis is in doubt, repeating the tests and examinations within a month may lead to increased information that proves the initial diagnosis was wrong and wrong, for example, stiffness and accumulation for the purpose of esophageal reflux. The ways of confirming the diagnosis as the lack of proper functioning of the active organs are to some extent related to the incompleteness and incorrectness of the chemical standard of estrogen and progesterone level, as well as the ways of complete measurement of the mucous components. In order to obtain the necessary information about the complete production of these hormones, a partial evaluation or all the sensitive tissues should be done. Changes in vaginal cells, mucus Cervix, basic temperature and compounds related to the inner lining of the uterus show the recent estrogenic or progesterone effect.. The most important period in which secretions and the inner membrane of the uterus change from the normal state of activity is one during adolescence and puberty and the other in old age. There is despair. Patients of female genital organs suffering from bleeding due to lack of proper activity. 10% .They are active members. In general, almost the majority of women suffer from such degrees. Proposed theories Disorders related to the mind and body are among the main causes.. is that the stability of the body parts through the nerve chain to the pituitary gland or changes in the diameter of the arteries in Biopsy help Bleeding without ovulation .

The ovaries or the inner membrane of the uterus are threatened. The inner membrane of the uterus can be detected in the office or by shaving on the first day of bleeding in the hospital, so that the part that shows the secretory changes before taking the sample on the background temperature may be practically important.. Observing the destruction of the mucous membrane of the neck is a sign of egg shedding. Bleeding from the inner membrane of the uterus during rapid reproduction is possible. It is practically important. Observing the destruction of the mucous membrane of the neck is a sign of egg shedding. Bleeding from the inner membrane of the uterus during rapid reproduction may be normal according to its amount, duration and sequence; However, when abnormal bleeding without histological changes Uterus or ovaries appear, most of the time the fall of the egg has been observed.. The prescription of the extract of the stimulating elements of the gland, which is currently commercially available, has been very effective in creating the desired ovarian stimulation in women.

The available preparation has an origin depending on the external placenta of the fetus or obtained from other animal organs use Inhuman extract is obtained. Estrogen-like non-steroidal compound, chlorothriacin, is known as clomiphene. Clomiphene has the power to disrupt the mucosal-ovarian balance in a way that causes ovulation in women. However, experience shows that it often results in the formation of a bag, and by the time this book is written in the United States, more research has been done on this hypothesis. Since there is no effective stimulation that results in ovulation, progesterone is prescribed to increase the secretion of the uterine lining and for more natural nourishment and shedding of the uterine lining. Holmström and others found that after Several types of intramuscular injection of progesterone together with the oil will trigger ovulation.. Irregular shedding of the endometrium with a cut more than five days after an attack of excessive bleeding or Continuous bleeding can be identified. Histological studies show that membrane leakage The inside of the uterus is scattered in the region of the endometrium..

McKelvey and Samuels proved that the long-term activity of the corpus luteum is one of the primary causes of this. It is a nuisance. Shaving is often followed by urea bleeding. Abnormal proliferation of the endometrium can be detected by biopsy or excision, and this condition may be the result of continuous estrogen use, or it may be accompanied by granulosa estrogen-producing cells or cancerous tumor cells. When this discomfort is due to non-neoplastic ovarian estrogen secretion, periodic administration of progesterone may be effective. . Excessive bleeding may occur without any obvious reason from the secretion of the inner lining of the uterus during menstrual periods for a normal period. Shaving is sometimes done for several periods for improvement. Progestin periodic treatment may be effective. Therapeutic measures: The four most important methods of treating uterine bleeding due to the lack of proper activity Active members are described below: Dilation and shaving It is not possible for abnormal bleeding to occur again for at least several months after dilatation and shaving.

Progestogens

injection50 to 100 mg of progesterone in ointment for four to seven days in the muscle before bleeding that has a favorable result may be used to regulate abnormal bleeding without ovulation. After three months of treatment, you should pay attention to the results. 5 mg Norlutit three times a day from the 15th to the 22nd day of menstruation. It may be effective. How the bleeding continued almost daily for an abnormally long time.

Kurd, the progesterone in the oil may stop the bleeding or reduce the bleeding for several days and result in sufficient shedding of the endometrium four to seven days after the termination. I used it. For the effect of progestin, reproduction is necessary depending on the inner lining of the uterus. Sufficient stimulation of estrogen should take place.

Estrogen- Diethylstilbestrol5 to 25 mg per day for twenty-five days, usually two to fifteen days after the bleeding stops. On the third day of bleeding, this treatment starts again and until twenty one. The day continues. After three courses of treatment, pay attention to the result. Excessive use of estrogen prevents egg from falling. If pregnancy is the patient's concern, this way of treatment is to the detriment of the patient. Progestin that is given in the second half of the menstrual period It does not prevent the egg from falling.

Estrogen and progestogen compounds

When they start on the fifth day of the cycle and continue for 20 days, it is possible to prevent the release of the egg, and with the increase in the menstrual flow, the secretion of the inner lining of the uterus also begins. A milligram of Enavid daily is usually effective. will be. 5 to 10 All these medical measures do not have the slightest effect in stabilizing the balance of the ovarian mucosa and are only used as a temporary treatment in the hope that the patient may improve on his own. are used. After a patient has given birth to several children or if infertility is observed, Hysterectomy may be effective in solving the problem of bleeding.. The necessary decision should be based on your strength Weak abnormal bleeding should be taken, lest these women who suffer from mental and physical discomforts They are fed up and cannot tolerate a hysterectomy.. When hormones are prescribed, androgenic production of ovarian hormones should be taken into account and adjusted for periodic changes, unless the regulation of secretion depends on the membrane.

Do not consider the inside of the uterus. If there is irregularity of ovarian activity and how to The sensitivity of the inner lining of the uterus has been damaged, it is not surprising if efforts are made in the field of treatment. An effective period did not happen and was not successful. Attention to abnormal uterine bleeding in patients of different ages The age of the patient can be matched with the causes of bleeding:

From birth to ten years old

Uterine bleeding related to the first four weeks of childbirth is due to the cessation of maternal estrogen, which disappears within a few days without the need for treatment.. damage as a result of wounding or wounding due to the presence of external factors in the vagina, usually the main cause of vaginal or vaginal bleeding.

When it grows up, it becomes more like a child. Vaginal bleeding may appear with precocious puberty. This situation is usually accompanied by puberty before the time of ovulation. With cystic growth, estrogen stimulation causes premature development of breasts and pubic hair. Bleeding related to the inner lining of the uterus has occurred and may later be replaced by ovulation. There are no traces of neoplazaria, and the child is normal. But as it continues to grow more intensely, both parents and children must confront the issue of early sexual advances.. Granulosa cell or theca cell tumors from the causes .Uterine bleeding in children is rare. Since these tumors may be dangerous, as long as the ovarian mass is palpable, the abdominal wall should be cut to obtain a correct diagnosis. Isolation is necessary if there is a neoplasm of the estrogen tube.. Uterine neoplasm in children. It is very rare. Bunch of grapes is a swelling of the middle layer of the mixed germ that may result in a more dangerous disease. In any case, it has been seen less that the affected patient can live more than one year. If there is cancer in the back

From ten to eighteen years old

All the causes related to the abnormal bleeding mentioned above should also be taken into consideration at this stage.. Careful and complete attention to the patient's records is necessary, and a physical and laboratory examination of the patient is unavoidable. Inconveniences related to hereditary blood clotting are likely to be seen in this group. As long as the hymen prevents a finger from entering, the examination will be performed correctly. Anesthesia may be used to prevent mental discomfort, in which case the possibility of a favorable examination is more extensive. After pregnancy, injury as a result of injury and organic causes are taken into consideration, the best diagnosis is the lack of proper functioning of active organs. Iron is emphasized for the elimination of anemia and jaundice, complete food abstinence, provision of necessary vitamin deficiency and accurate weight review. If the bleeding is heavy or continuous, estrogen is prescribed to temporarily stop the bleeding. If bleeding stops, to ensure duration Stop using progestins such as Neurotit.. As long as these effective elements did not appen, there is no other choice but to shave while unconscious. This method usually leads to treatment and From eighteen to forty years old

Pregnancy and its complications are usually the cause of abnormal bleeding in this stage.. As long as there is a possibility of pregnancy, until the complete examination and confirmation of the suspected situation of invasion of the uterus, it is prevented, if the uterus is small and there is bleeding, shaving is an unavoidable thing.

Pelvic infections, endometrial abscess, endometriosis, abscesses Ovarian and blood disorders need more attention and diagnosis of the general condition of the body based on studies. It becomes more obvious. Bleeding based on the inactivity of active organs is one of the main issues of this.

Over forty years old

The possibility of a dangerous disease situation should always be kept in mind.. Since pregnancy is rarely noticed by the patient, hysterectomy is the best treatment if the abnormal bleeding is recurring. To prevent incomplete treatment and especially to prevent forgiveness and It is easy to imagine the effective treatment of cancer, the diagnosis must be based on a solid and accurate basis..Radiation therapy, which was once used to treat and control the harmless stage of uterine bleeding, has given way to hysterectomy in the United States for the following reasons:(1) the diagnosis becomes more accurate (2) it leads to protection of ovarian activity (3) possibility It limits the development of uterine cancer.

After stopping menstruation

One or more years before the last period, the slightest bleeding is a sign of the need for cancer screening.. Cytological tests, biopsy and study related to the inner membrane of the uterus are necessary. Hemorrhoids related to endometrium related to aging along with endometrial tumors and vaginal tumors related to aging, especially trichomoniasis, are harmless causes.

Painful menstruation

When painful menstruation occurs from the beginning of menstruation, it is divided into the primary or natural period.. Usually, there is no explanatory reason. Secondary painful menstruation after months and years of Menstrual cramps may occur and dramatic changes may be seen depending on the discomfort.. The pain may be due to the following factors: (1) uterine contractions (2) continuous pain in such People, which is thought to be the cause" Blood concentration in the muscles". Weakness, loss of appetite, confusion, vomiting, sweating, nausea and headache may also accompany this discomfort, any or all of these conditions may be present especially in the initial painful menstruation. Often They will be inconvenienced, but only a few of them need it.

Women have more or less menstruation. They are treated. picture- 20 exercises for painful menstruation. A - The patient stands well next to the wall to be able to easily lean the left elbow on the wall parallel to the shoulder. B - Side view of the style It shows putting the hand on the opposite bail. C - The pelvis is bent forward, while in this position, the patient rubs his left shoulder against the wall, kneeling.. The same action is also true for the surety It is repeated. D-The patient stands against the wall and leans his elbows on the wall. E.F - The pelvis is bent forward to the extent that the joint of the pelvic bone contacts the wall. The heels of the feet are stuck to the ground and the knees are stretched.. Scientific motivation- Painful menstruation may be due to one or more reasons.

Psychological causes

Ignoring the importance and purpose of menstruation or socializing with menstruating women. Painful, even if it is psychologically weak, it may cause physical symptoms.. It may be useful to suggest following the patient's usual activities or specific exercises..

Explanatory disorders

Cervical canal stenosis, congenital or acquired, can be called less discomfort anyway.. Intrauterine clotting or shedding of large pieces of the uterine lining and intervention in shedding .It may be important. Bending or malposition of the organs with apparently congenital origin.

It is not known. The pain from the back part of the uterus is very severe in some women. Maybe this is a sign. There are disturbances in the chain of organs.

Conditions related to pathology

Endometrial edema, pelvic swelling, and uterine or ovarian neoplasms are possible causes of menstruation. Painful neck. Pregnancy changes accompanied by bleeding should not be confused with painful menstruation. Abdominal, bladder, urinary tract, intestinal pain may start at the same time as menstruation..1-Treatment Since painful menstruation has intrinsic symptoms instead of sexual discomfort, if the necessary treatment is done for the part that causes painful menstruation, it can be It provided peace and relief to the patient. When there is no organ or organ cause, the discomfort of the active organ is top It can be solved in various ways:

Painful initial menstrual pressure usually begins with periodic ovulation..Ovulation using estrogen2 mg of diethylacetylbestrol or its heme row drug every day, from the beginning of the second day of menstruation and continuing for twenty one days, causes the eruption of menstruation "without twist". It can be two to three days each time He repeated the same thing as usual.

Anesthetizing elements such as Idrisal, Fanafen or Darwin or their combination is possible. The reason for the extraordinary pain relief. Less strong drugs are used. Codeine, a second tablet5 Aspirin tablets have solved the problem of addiction. Neck dilatation may be a relief. Pregnancy is usually effective in relieving this pain. Marriage, from the point of view of physical change or the benefits of sexual intercourse, is it possible to be effective in the absence of discomfort. be. Cutting the sensitive legs of the uterus in the areas before the sacrum or the uterus of the sacrum only in the case of women suffering from severe pain when other methods have not been effective, or It is not enough, it will be done. Excitement before menstruation in a patient suffering from a mental disorder is likely.

The symptoms of frequent excitement before menstruation are It will show itself and reduce the joy and happiness of more cheerful women.. Depression, B Cramps, abdominal cramps, headache, back pain, confusion and slight swelling may be seen before menstruation.. Changes in the balance of electrical corruption and sodium increase may occur. This situation leads to water retention and weight gain. Depending on the inner membrane of the uterus, it causes defects. Limiting salt intake and using diuretics have been effective in some women..It is very traditional. As the problem of pain becomes more complicated, it is possible to use anesthetic and pain medication. Analgesic drugs may cause symptoms to calm down in the patient. Severe symptoms and the occurrence of general disability should be considered for psychological treatment evaluation, and possibly against climate change, induction, suggestions and treatments through compassion, which are usually less uncomfortable in patients with less discomfort, are effective. They do not show practicality.

Painful intercourse forms or intercourse pain may be partial and permanent, or this pain may be be so severe that it makes its operation unbearable. the cause- The causes of painful reaction include the following points: Irregularities Defective hymen and missing vagina are seen more than all.. walled vagina (bivaginal) usually does not cause obstruction, but it may obstruct production and when Intercourse is torn apart. The presence of a thick hymen may cause frequent pain and impossibility of intercourse.. If the clinical dilation is very painful, cutting the hymen and sometimes a part of the hymen Because of his calmness, he becomes sick.

Vaginal cysts, vaginal cysts, Bartholin's gland swelling, scan gland swelling and urinary tract cysts They can be the cause of penetration into the vagina. Scratches caused by surgical incisions or dental sutures sometimes leave painful effects and need to be cut to relieve this pain. Defective occlusal suture causes the narrowing of the forge. In the same way, surgery and vaginal suture are possible to reduce its size. will be.Intra-pelvic diseases for possible infection, endometrial tumor or neoplasia It is when a man's penis descends too much and causes pain for a woman.. With the 3rd degree of uterine prolapse, the ovaries are located in the cold sac and so on. If the male penis descends enough, it causes a wound.. Thinning and drying of the organs due to aging, post-radiation weight loss, vaginal dryness, or vaginal dryness due to leukoplakia may cause the loss of vaginal size to such an extent that The cause of pain is during intercourse.

Psychological origin

When the vulva and vagina are soft, the reflex action of women causes the muscles around the vagina to contract in such a way that this member is protected.. This contraction is possible according to the degree Increase the pain. When there is no physical reason for painful intercourse, spasm.A vaginal issue can be considered as a result of fear.. This fear is to such an extent that the patient is not present to place the head of the special shower tube in his vagina or the doctor to put even a finger in his vagina.

The doctor's indoctrination about the natural development of the genital organ and gentle examination of the genital organ may cause the gradual expansion of the patient's genital organ. some of Patients can overcome their fear by using the penis enlargement device.. explanations Regarding the contraction and expansion of the vaginal muscles, it may be useful in solving the problem of the patient's fear.. Sometimes local vaginal spasm appears as brain and psychological disorders, which is better. In such cases, he got help from a psychiatrist.

Sexual coldness

The lack of a strong sexual feeling in a woman during her period is not as debatable and important as a man, because only the state of menopause is necessary for culture and insemination leading to pregnancy.. The strong sexual feeling and the outburst of lust that follows it does not have the slightest effect on the process of fertilization.

Its presence and increase doubles the possibility of pregnancy and the pleasure and satisfaction of married life.. From the history of sexual disorders, it appears that completely normal and healthy women do not have the slightest sexual feelings for the first few months or years of marriage, or this feeling is very weak in them, and in this case, it is not until after the birth of one or several children. has it. The opposite effect of sexual feeling usually depends a lot on the way of sexual activity and the satisfying intercourse depending on the nature of the woman. This simple fact is very important because it always becomes the primary basis of all the incompatibilities and separations in the family, and it is when the husband or wife does not enjoy each other as it should and they engage in sexual intercourse. To depression and dissatisfaction .It becomes a party. Some of the patients, due to the neglect of their parents, have a wrong idea of its functional role in life. They have their own marriage. These patients need instructions for their sexual issues.

The doctor's orders should be used by the patient along with the reading of books and articles in this field.. Fortunately, many useful books in this category have been edited and are available, and the best of them are Marital Love by Marie Stopes and Fearlessness. Gender by the pen of S. O He mentioned Levin and John Gilmore.

Treatment

It is necessary for the doctor to find out the main cause of the problem as far as possible and encourage the patient to express his thoughts and opinions about this issue.. In most cases, it is the husband's fault that they neglect the method of preparing a woman for full enjoyment of this act. In other cases, the patient has a deep hatred inside him, which is either due to the imperfect teachings of sex or the existence of events in the patient's past life and environment, which is the cause of the patient's hatred of the male gender in general. There may be reasons specific to the husband, and this reason may be due to the woman's feeling of inadequacy or other habits in the man.

Such cases can often be treated by doctors who have little knowledge of psychiatry, and in more difficult cases, it is better to go to marriage counseling specialists or to a psychologist. Consult with a qualified doctor, because with the delay in this case and putting off this issue today to tomorrow. It is possible to bear the damages of compensation.. General treatment including eliminating any kind of discomfort and disease of the member as much as possible.

It is. By using tonics, by changing the living environment, by avoiding the discomforts of life, exhausting work and also excessive sexual intercourse, rest plays a major role in the treatment of this discomfort, because in such a situation, the husband and wife are in turmoil. The city is far away and the winged and cheerful style is only interested in the pleasure of using the fresh air and also in a peaceful environment. They lose their enjoyment. Secretion disorders sometimes cause a decrease in sexual pleasure.. The most famous exudative discomfort in The patients who complained about this condition were due to the lack of activity of the thyroid gland..

By providing the necessary thyroid, if the reason for the lack of pleasure from sexual intercourse is exclusively the lack of thyroid, the issue of dissatisfaction with its relationship will be eliminated. Hypopituitarism and hypovariance in some cases There have been major causes. R. G. Crosen reminds them that estrogen and testosterone in Some combinations have been effective in certain cases. Oral or vaginal drug treatment operations should be a trial first, if the test result is successful, subcutaneous treatment It may be used.

Infertility

Determining the cause of sterility and fruitlessness requires knowledge of all aspects of the science of women's reproductive organs, and it is a test of knowledge.. The information in this chapter ID is mentioned only to emphasize the importance of its main points.. definition-The types of infertility and their definition are as follows: 1-Primary infertility - pregnancy has never been seen.

The main points of infertility manifestations in women

These points are close to the majority of women suffering from infertility if they are read completely.. 9- Hohner's test four hours or less before intercourse close to ovulation, the reason for the study Sperms are found in the cervical mucus and their quantity and activity are determined.. This study cannot be included in the analysis and complete analysis of sperm, which includes (a) volume, viscosity and stickiness, turbidity, and pH of the fluid depending on semen, (b) morphology, motility, and complete sperm count, and (c) determination Existence or lack of leucocytes and bacteria. - 10 tests depending on the evolution of PBI, BMR); Blood cholesterol and possible glucose tolerance tests It is necessary to ensure the desired power of the thyroid11. Determination of FSH and 17-ketosteroid depending on the urine in rare cases with clinical investigations. will take. Treatment: Inflammatory or obstructive diseases of the vulva, vagina, or cervix should be eradicated if possible. will be. The procedure is as follows: 1-Estimating the time of insemination by predicting ovulation. 2- Abstinence of the husband for five days or more to collect more adult sperms. 3- Avoidance of the patient from showering and other things that may cause damage to the sperms (in part) It is necessary to douche before sexual intercourse(4) A woman lies down like an open arch for half an hour after intercourse (this action is the reason for the rest).

The sperm remains in the vagina, which is sometimes useful.(5- Confirmation of necessary nutrition; in case of need to regulate anemia and the level of necessary vitamins in food, maybe It is necessary to lose weight and prescribe additional vitamins..6- Necessary exercises and rest, induction and other psychological measures may be effective. or a thyroid extract pill as a trial without The treatment of the internal secretions of the glands is included Laboratory evidence of increased secretion activity is recommended.. Low amount of estrogen, 0.25 mg Diethylstilbestrol daily for twenty one days, when the bleeding attack is repeated. It may be used in case of diagnosis of mucosal bleeding stasis.. Progesterones, both natural and synthetic, should be restarted in case of bleeding during ovulation.

The above treatment efforts may not be fruitful, but if they are used in the necessary amount, they will certainly not harm the general health of the patient. Hormonal treatment to increase thyroid activity and adrenal gland activity deficits may be directed towards Showing infertility is also effective. Entering gas or air in the neck tube is sometimes effective from a therapeutic point of view. As the normal blood pressure was obtained in three periods, the repetition of this test is ineffective.

Tuboplasty may be curative in selected patients, considering that according to the report, the opening is about 50% of patients and only 25% in general. Surgery is scheduled, there is a possibility of pregnancy.. The best time for tuboplasty It is when abdominal wall incision is done for other purposes.. Pipe blockage Mostly as a result of uterine tubercle amas which has caused damage to the tubular mucous membrane skin and Tubular muscle tissue is damaged. Since the fallopian tube must deliver the egg to the uterus.

Openness alone cannot be effective. Separation of myosoma with the help of surgery and cutting Areas affected by endometrial tumors are rarely prescribed just for the purpose of infertility treatment, but since this operation is done to relieve symptoms and pain and to reduce the volume of accumulation, there is a possibility that the patient will be able to solve this problem. to be fertile. Before removing the myometrium with surgical help and cutting the areas affected by endometrial tumors, a complete study and careful xamination of the husband and wife is absolutely necessary. Artificial insemination is the use of the husband's sperm, which can be done in a patient who is infertile for no apparent reason, and if the husband's sperm count is semi-normal. Legal and ethical issues of medical professionals The results of this action were not satisfactory.

The reproductive system prompts women to refrain from using the sperm of another person against the patient's request.. If pregnancy does not appear for several years, despite the fact that there is no obvious reason and sign for infertility despite careful examinations, the best way to strengthen the marital bond is to choose an adopted child. There are many husbands and wives who live without children for years without having any reason for infertility. Infertility of the organ related to the active organs of the body sometimes He needs a psychiatrist. different disorders

The age of despair

Menopause is a period in which a gradual decrease in ovarian activity is observed.. The attack is before menopause and the end is months or years after it. Its outward signs are the reduction of ovarian volume and the reduction of estrogenic stimulation changes. After the bleeding stops, the activity dries up The reproductive organs, the breasts, are revealed by microscopic gross changes.. At the age of desperation, which appears by itself, menses are less frequent and less frequent before they stop completely. The amount of blood on it is reduced a little. the cause Menstruation can happen in several ways:

Spontaneously and involuntarily:

The ovaries are unable to respond to the stimulation of the gland. The number of driving hormones. A bag increases after menopause because the estrogen level still stops. It has not been received.

Hysterectomy:

Despite the fact that there is no effect of shedding on the inner lining of the uterus, the ovaries after It continues its activity even after hysterectomy.. Estrogen deficiency before reaching the patient I don't notice the age of menarche. Two-way separation: When the main source of estrogen and progesterone are separated, Bleeding due to the inner membrane of the uterus does not occur.. Changes depending on cytology and histology, despite the fact that in young women, estrogens and progesterones are in small amounts by The glands are produced by the kidneys and appear in the vagina.. Ovarian radiation: deep

X-ray treatment of the ovaries or sending radium in the vagina and uterus to the amount Coffee causes ovarian dryness. Symptoms: Almost the majority of women have symptoms that appear with age.

Treatment for the cause Disorders that appear in It as necessary for 15% of patients. Sudden hot waves that the patient feels all overedness: It has especially affected the upper chest and face areas.. Redness of the skin is possible It has appeared and there is sweating. These changes originally started from the veins, and The most important symptoms of old age are despair. Since redness appears both in men and in women with regular menstruation, it is obvious that the main cause is lack of It cannot be estrogen. Psychological disturbances may be the cause of redness, but As it is noticed in the study of women at the age of despair, this situation is the most documented. The guide for severe disorders is the age of despair.

Anger and anxiety:

The main symptoms are bruises, headache, insomnia, confusion and dizziness. Heart palpitations and chills are also common.. With a little attention, you can find that this Symptoms have psychological roots. In the psychological examination of women in this period, it should be noted that there are many points. and the numerous factors that cause the occurrence of women in this period, it should be noted that there are many points and factors that cause their occurrence, the importance of which is as follows: (1) pregnancy is no longer possible or is not desired by the patient, (2) physical strength is decreasing, and (3) the issue of the decline of the sexual attraction of the female organ may increase due to the following two reasons: (a) Children's growth and leave .

The freshness of a woman's youth creates inconsistency and bad promises and maybe betrayal.. Irregularity in menstruation: which continues from the lack of bleeding to the cessation of bleeding. A short period of stopping the patient's bleeding suggests a possible pregnancy. Despite the fact that the reduction of zinc blood during menstruation is a natural thing, some patients have menstrual bleeding. nose stain It often scares the patient about the possibility of cancer and so arrange: The patient's personal complaint of menopause cannot be the real cause of the diagnosis. The physical examination of the patient should show the lack of estrogenic stimulation of the breast, vulva, vaginal mucosa, and uterus Lest severe discomfort be ignored. with blood loss and Intramuscular bleeding of patients at this age is enough to cause an unavoidable cancer.. Normal cytology studies are necessary; Repetition of biopsy depending on the endometrium and incision for diagnosis, if necessary, is a research basis. How is the effect of neoplasia No, the remedy is bleeding due to the natural inactivity of the active organs.. The intense phase of flushing that causes discomfort is usually relieved by a small amount of estrogen. A milligram of premarin daily, one-half or one milligram of diethylstilbestrol 1/25 will be. On a daily basis, it is possible to use Green Blot and other pros of the combination of androgens and estrogens in confinement and prevention of redness on the condition that there is less possibility for Uterine bleeding and mammary glands go away. It is also possible to prescribe the use of medicine orally.

The method of treatment through a reduced food regimen has been approved.. Stuart Taylor from Proponents of this method are cycles in which estrogen is given for three weeks and one week off. becomes, and this work is in view of the defects of the possibility of falling depending on the inner membrane of the uterus.. Undoubtedly, in case of lack of uterus, this type of treatment is not necessary.. To monitor the types Symptoms that have a psychological origin, the full understanding of the patient is of the first importance..

Psychological treatment includes climate change, inference of the patient, indoctrination and guidance and driving the patient to the things he is interested in and the reward of good deeds such as taking care of grandchildren, paying attention to charity institutions. Works religious, charitable works, entertainment, etc.. Use of small amounts of tranquilizers Phenobarbital may be extremely effective in reducing the patient's worry and anxiety, and the reason. The patient will get more sleep. Reactive depression may occur in women at this age. When this situation occurs in a severe state, treatment and complete psychological care is necessary. Estrogen prescription is not very effective in this group of patients. Unnatural tenderness and Androgen causes temporary relief, but the radiologic changes return again..

The pain around the joints is related to estrogen deficiency; Anyway, so is estrogen Only because of this inconvenience, it is recommended to be extremely careful.. Except in the cases of vaginal cysts related to old age, the prescription of estrogen during menopause should not be associated with mucosal side effects. Mahbli will meet. Redness can often be treated without the necessary skin aging. Vaginal mucous membrane was monitored and prevented. Deficiency or lack of sexual desire is related to various factors during a person's life, so it is very difficult to be sure and confirm the effect of age on this psychological work. There are women who still maintain their sexual desire or have just reached it before menopause. Estrogen is rarely effective in increasing libido. Increased thyroid activity may appear before menopause and in contrast. A small amount of thyroid extract by mouth has side effects; However, this method is less effective in solving the problem of adipose tissue in inappropriate places. will be. It is better to fix this condition with the help of diet and exercise. The role of the breast in the diagnosis of female discomfort. Breast examination should be considered not only for the purpose of discharge, but also for the detection of neoplasia. As soon as possible, is important.

Pain in the mammary gland

Breast pain is a pain that most women who refer to gynecology specialists. Representatives complain about it. Mild breast tenderness before menstruation is more important than its frequency. It results naturally. The presence and persistence of tenderness after menstruation should be considered as a possible sign of other discomforts. The cystic disease of fibroid breast has been seen a lot. This disease is the cause .

The increase in nodal glands is similar to "Wavy" comes.

This is the situation .A little more than the cancerous tumors have occurred and it should be noted that the cancer may have started from an infected breast to become a fibroid cyst, and coincidentally, due to the fact that the patient was previously under examination, the breast cancer was diagnosed early.. A little tenderness of the breast. A day from the patient may be effective in calming the patient. To relieve less breast pain Estrogen and androgen are prescribed.

As the possibility of "nerve swelling" goes, painkillers and Vitamin B complex may be used.. Bags : When the patient is suspicious of having a bag in the breast, if the bags are observed in the breast a few weeks after giving birth, or the accumulation is felt in a free and circular manner in the breast.. It is possible to remove this free accumulation. These wounds can be removed by anesthetizing and artificial respiration of the patient. This method of treatment has been effective in many patients. Accumulations Residual or recurrent need to be cut.

Hard accumulations

They cut the hard lumps out of the body for fear that the cancer may not be detectable in the early stages.. A complete cut practically requires the patient to be anesthetized. In some patients suffering from cancer, especially those patients who have moved cancer, isolation or enough radiation to destroy the ovarian activity for the patient's comfort and convenience. In addition, the reason for increasing the life span of the patient is.

Bleeding

Bleeding from the tip of the breast is a sign of the need for a cytology study and often a full breast examination..

back pain

Back pain, pain related to the sacrum, or areas related to the sacrum and long intestine are usually discomforts that women who refer for examinations related to gynecological diseases express.. In most of these women, the least effect of pelvic diseases is not observed. The distribution of back pain and especially the pain related to the sacral bone in female disorders has been discussed in its own place. Back pain related to before menstruation and other apparently related types.

It is due to changes in the condition and blood circulation of the pelvis.. Predominance of blood or its concentration in the muscle, maybe It was accompanied by swelling and may be the primary mechanism.. It should not be forgotten that laziness and weakness or mental disorders may also follow. In order to understand the possible causes of back pain in women, the following points should not be forgotten, diseases of joint corruption; Muscle aches; increasing the ease of movement of the joints related to the sacrum and long intestine, tearing of the surface between two vertebrae, difficulty sitting, standing, and sleeping; in front of the bending of a bead on another seal, and finally Shortening of the lower extremity, all of which lead to a dark curvature of the back from the side..

points of forensic medicine in the science of female genital disorders

Issues related to forensic medicine in the practice of female genital disorders can be divided into two stages.. The first stage is a case where the doctor is prosecuted for the treatment of the mistake, and the second stage is a case where the female genital discomfort specialist is summoned to the court to testify in special cases. The danger that threatens doctors in recent years is wrong treatment, which is often not based on solid reasons. According to the latest figures, one out of every seven doctors in the United States has been sued. The same ratio in New York and the District of Columbia is one in five and in California one in four.. Although most of it.

The lawsuits have been based on the existence of these major damages to the doctor in particular and the medical science in general; Therefore, it is obligatory for every doctor to avoid being contaminated by such things as it is written by Regan and Moritz in the book of Forensic Medicine. It is: The basis of the work is that the relationship between the doctor and the patient should be based on mutual trust.. a doctor Sharif, Hazeq, must be sure with his conscience that as long as he is doing a worthy and permissible action and is free of any kind of violation, he will never be objected and prosecuted leading to a scandal and will not be sentenced to pay damages. Spend a lot of time In order to enforce the sentence, in order to be released from punishment, he will not have.

The list below of the main cases of error treatment and how to avoid them as necessary information in the book It is printed above: 1- Never criticize another doctor unless you have all the necessary facts, and In such a situation, it is better not to talk to the patient in this category.. 2- Do not leave the patient before completing the examination. Recently, a midwife was brought to court After examining the patient, it is decided to go to the hospital after other work and as a result, before Arriving at the delivery room, the patient is discharged.. 3- All the possibilities of the necessary means should be used for the necessary diagnosis, now this diagnosis is for Cancer or pregnancy or other cases. 4- Never promise to improve. 5- Be very careful in choosing assistants and regularly monitor their assigned duties. 6- In cases of surgery, a written consent signed by the husband and wife in the presence of two witnesses. The letter of consent should include any action that may be taken during the surgery .as correct. 7-Make sure that you can accept any care responsibilities after surgery.

8- Even when you remove the uterus, do not promise the patient to be sterility and sterility. After Hysterectomy also resulted in pregnancy again.. 9- Don't try to sterilize the patient unless medical reasons require this action and Always consider the social provisions of the law of the region where you perform such action. have. Before doing this, inform two consultant doctors for this action. 10- Never feel free from responsibility for absurd reasons. 11- The issue of artificial insemination of the sperm of a second person other than the husband is a case that has a certain legal status. does not have. 12- When examining a patient, a nurse must always be present. In this list, only some important points have been mentioned, but it must be accepted that it is very incomplete. For more information, it is better to refer to the original book of Forensic Medicine by Qalam Morgan and Refer to Mortiz. The reader can also read the summary of the article published in the magazine. The evening post has come under the title of medicine and society.. The second stage is when the doctor is called as a witness. There are many cases in which the medical person has written an invitation to testify or surrender based on the belief about the genitals.

It becomes a person. These testimonials are usually and simply a report on the description, physiology, anesthesiology, diagnosis, treatment and prediction of the period of unhappiness. The doctor is forced to face it in his daily work.. But there are cases that Normal diagnosis or treatment of an infinite disease are of little importance, but when they are brought to the court, their real importance is revealed.. Therefore, when a doctor starts a job in which there is the least possibility of being dragged to the court, he should use the utmost care. Medical testimony is usually used to confirm or substantiate claims of defamation or violent adultery. The accusation of defamation has been seen a lot. Taylor states that between each of the twelve stages of dishonor that The court has been drawn up, only one case was rape with actual violence.. Some of these cases of defamation brought to the court were caused by mistake, such as child, child and Extortion or revenge, or other purposes have been carried out.. The problem that the doctor faces after the examination during the examination period is to make sure whether or not sexual intercourse has taken place.

Also, proof of disease transmission should be considered and presented. The effects of resistance and struggle in violent adultery are very important.. Trying to find a man's sperm on the body or inside the woman's body is not ineffective in obtaining results.. Usually, male sperm or spermatozoa are released from the vagina six to twelve hours after sexual intercourse, or they are decomposed, which also varies.

 If the duration of sexual intercourse and examination is more than six hours, the chance of finding dried sperm on the patient's body or clothes is more than on the vagina. Evidence of wound and abnormal pressure should also be taken into consideration. Type issue An existing disease, especially gonorrhea, syphilis, or chancre, and how it is spread and whether it is still contagious. Yes or no, there are issues that have different legal aspects under different conditions; For example, in divorce, child custody, alimony, or damage claims against individuals . The following questions arise: What kind of disease do you have? What are the main points of your diagnosis based on? In your opinion, has the treating doctor shown the necessary accuracy and skill in diagnosis or not? In your opinion, did the treating doctor use the necessary care and skill in the treatment or not? Before answering this question, try to ignore the law of the state in which these questions are asked of you.

The importance of placing foreign bodies in the patient's abdomen until the question The court is not drawn as it should be, and it may not be clear to the doctor.. It is important here Try not to leave surgical instruments and rods in the peritoneal cavity during surgery. And this very important topic from the point of view of its valuable points in a detailed explanation by the pen of Krosen and Krosen. It has come under the title of placement of foreign bodies in the abdomen. Issues related to midwifery are not discussed here. For complete information on medical issues Refer to the book Doctor and Patient and Law written by Stetler and Mortiz..

Bibliography

1-Main, Denise M.: Obstetrics and Gynecology, Department of Obstetrics,

 Washington University 2014

2- Leister, Susan: surgery in women, Medical school, London University,2012

3- Madison, Simon: obstetrics, Medical school, London university 2019

4-Winson, Helen: Gynecology and obstetrics, Medical school, University of London, 2011

5-Maloney, Susan: Internal Medicine, Florida State University Brown, Miller, Specia

 Diseases, London University, 2010

6-CFP Wharton AR Archer, Pediatrics, London

University, 2019
7- Textbook of Pediatrics, London WBsaundrs.2009,

www.ingramcontent.com/pod-product-compliance
Lightning Source LLC
LaVergne TN
LVHW091226180726
843490LV00006B/1959